BARGAIN

MW01115506

One Family's Account of Navigating the World of Healthcare without Insurance

By Jennifer Heyns

Disclaimer

Table of Contents

Chapter 1: Why and Why Not?

The Whys?
Why the Book?

There are many reasons why I chose to tackle the issue of living without health insurance in such a public way. First and foremost because there are about 47 million Americans living without health insurance right now and that number is growing. It's growing because so many people just can't afford health insurance. It's expensive and let's face it, if you're self-employed, unemployed or your employer just doesn't offer it for free or at a subsidized rate it can be an overwhelming expense. Not to mention that while you're paying large sums of money in the name of monthly premiums you don't always get what you pay for. Many people have learned this the hard way paying years' worth of premiums to HMOs only to find that when something terrible happens the insurance company finds a way not to cover the medical expenses incurred or drops them like the proverbial hot potato.

So, I write this book in the hopes of helping people, regardless of insurance status. I want to help people who don't have health insurance learn how to find the best care they can get at affordable prices, but also to let them know that they're not alone. You are NOT alone. There's no shame in not having health insurance, the only shame is in not getting proper care when you need it and not being able to afford it if you do. The shame is in being scared of medical disasters, doctors and hospitals because of the stigma attached to not having insurance or because of possible financial ruin. The shame is in letting fear guide your medical care choices. And the biggest shame is in letting the capitalistic ploys of HMOs and the medical profession instill shame and fear into you when there's absolutely nothing wrong with living without health insurance. In fact, not too many decades ago health insurance was nonexistent and every person dealt with their healthcare choices on their own, just as 47 million of us do today.

The second reason I wanted to write this book was to keep people who DO have health insurance in the loop. There are so many things you take for granted when you have health insurance. I know. I used to be one of those people. I knew what my monthly premiums and doctor visit co-pays cost, but that was pretty much it. Everything else I left up to my HMO to deal with. Insurance customers cannot afford to let their HMO dictate their care and the costs associated with it. I truly believe that the reason why doctor bills, hospital bills and health insurance premiums keep rising to astonishing new heights is because collectively we're just not being vigilant enough.

My eyes were opened for the first time when my family canceled our health insurance policy. It's amazing how watchful you become when every single thing you do associated with the healthcare of your family will be paid for out of your own pocket. All of a sudden you become blindingly aware of what things cost. You learn to question everything. You learn to rely on yourself and your research skills. There are so many things that I've learned since we've been living without health insurance. What kills me though, is that I should have been this way all along. I should have been questioning everything, relying on my own instincts, doing lots of research and acting like our healthcare was in my own hands even when we had an HMO backing us.

So, I write this book with the hopes that not only can I help people, but also so I can educate people, regardless of whether they have health insurance or not, because healthcare is a huge problem in this nation and until we all hold ourselves accountable for the care we seek and receive and the costs we allow to be incurred then we will never be able to bring our system into check. And isn't that one of the foundations of American life? A system of checks and balances. WE the people need to start checking and balancing the system. The scales have been tipped too far in the opposing direction. It's time to be accountable and responsible and to hold those in power to the same standards. I do believe in change, it's a good thing, and it's inevitable, and if we work together we can change things for the betterment of society. We shouldn't need government to step in and make new laws to "protect" us because, let's be honest here, whenever Big Brother steps in, it very rarely works out in the favor of the average American citizen. If we really want the benefits to come to us, we have to force it upon ourselves to see it through.

Lastly, I wrote this book because I have so many stories to share; lessons I've learned, information I've gathered, experiences I've been through. I'm not a doctor, a nurse, or an employee of any medical organization. I'm just an average American, like you. But I've learned to live a happy, nice life without worrying about health insurance or medical costs. I've learned to successfully take care of my family's healthcare without health insurance and without fear and shame.

Why Me?
I am an ordinary woman. I work from home as a writer, I have a husband, two sons, a dog and a house to keep up with along with the usual stack of bills.

What I don't have is health insurance.

Why? Because my husband and I decided not to.

Why? After our first son was born we decided that I would have the luxury of quitting my job and staying home to take care of him. Our health insurance, which we had through the company I was working for, covered my family through my maternity leave and was extended another 18 months through the COBRA program. By the end of COBRA we were on our own in terms of medical care, which panicked me terribly as a new mother.

Immediately we picked up the tab for our own family policy through Kaiser Permanente. We were never thrilled with the fact that Kaiser is an all-inclusive medical care company – you have virtually no choice in facilities, doctors, treatments, etc. – but it was the most affordable insurance at the time and finances dictated all facets of our life then.

We soon welcomed a second son into our family and were delighted to find that he, like his brother, was healthy as could be. Soon after, though, we fell into very difficult times, financially. We were a one-income family and that one income was unsteady at best.

My husband owns his own one-man construction company. Being self-employed is an on-going struggle in any case, but we had been doing great with two large contracts that came through very close together. Unfortunately, both customers defaulted on their contracts, one right after the other. Our business and personal finances went into an immediate tailspin. As do all good crews, worth their weight, when the ship starts to sink, we began throwing our excess baggage overboard.

The first financial cut was made in the entertainment category – no more eating out, going to movies and the like. It was not enough to save us. Then we started cutting back on our bills; no more cable television, no more trash pick-up (we could haul our own muck to the dump, thank you very much!), no more heating the house with propane while the wood stove sat idle all winter, no more long-distance plan when our cell phones would do the same for less. We kept cutting and sacrificing, but it still wasn't enough.

After a careful review of the rest of our expenses we determined that there really wasn't anything else we could cut (we would have cut the credit card bills out, but Visa declined to see it that way). Then my husband asked what we were paying in health insurance premiums – I was stunned into silence, which, for those of you who know me, is not an easy feat. I didn't even want to answer him; there was no way we could live without health insurance. Was he crazy? Here I was with two baby boys – BOYS, you know the sex that's prone to roughhousing, horsing around and generally getting beat up and broken just by virtue of their gender. He persisted. Against my better judgment I admitted that we were paying nearly $600 a month for health insurance. *"And when was the last time any of us went to the doctor?"* asked Mr. Smarty-pants. I have learned in our decade plus of marriage that when he gets like that, the only way to appease him is to get out all of the paperwork and start crunching the numbers. What I found, however, did not appease him. What it did do was shock and amaze us both. That year, which was circa 2002, we had spent more than $8600 in medical expenses. This is not the shocking part – the kicker was that $7000 of that figure was spent in health insurance premiums alone.

7

Upon closer inspection we realized that each of us had only been to the doctor once that year for our annual physicals. We had also been to the dentist for routine cleanings, check-ups, x-rays and a filling or two; none of which were covered by our health insurance plan so even though we were paying our premiums, we were paying these expenses out of pocket anyway. We also paid about $230 for birth control pills and other prescriptions that year, above what was covered by our health policy. What hit us hardest was realizing that the $7000 we had paid in premiums that year was really just to cover four routine physicals with our family practitioner which equates to $1750 per visit!

As amazed as I was by these realizations, I was still not convinced that we should drop our coverage. As with most mothers, my biggest fear was that one, or both, of my children would become injured or contract a life-threatening disease and that we would not be able to afford the best care for them. (There was, of course, also that nagging fear that the $180 spent on birth control would be in vain and that there would soon be *three* kids to keep from breaking legs and spraining wrists!)

What finally convinced me was a combination of my husband's voice of reason and a bit of research on my part. My husband rationalized that the money we were GIVING to the health insurance company was really just money down the drain – money we didn't have to give. Not only would that money be better spent helping to get us out of debt, but it would serve us better to invest that money on our own behalf and then, God forbid, should something catastrophic happen, we would pay for it out of pocket from our nest egg.

It's now been several years since we decided for the daring lifestyle of being health insuranceless and we haven't regretted it yet. In fact, on many occasions we have been thankful for our choice. Being independent of the health insurance industry we have gone about our healthcare in a much more cautious, resourceful, conscientious and curious manner and have learned a great deal about the medical marketplace.

After my son's oral surgery in January 2007, which constituted weeks of grueling research on my part to ensure my son's safety and well-being before allowing any procedures to take place, my husband suggested that I write a magazine article about what I had learned. He put a little bug in my ear that I had a social responsibility to share my experiences and knowledge on the topic of healthcare with the other millions of Americans who do not have health insurance, whether by choice or not, as well as with those who do have health care. For those who have medical insurance – I would begrudge you nothing, you deserve the best care you can get as well, but you, too, should be aware of some of the lessons I have learned so that you can decide if your policy is worthwhile as well as to be alert to the "real" costs of your healthcare.

My goal is to teach everyone how to navigate the healthcare industry successfully; how to find the right healthcare professionals, how to determine what the proper care should encompass, how to ensure proper billing takes place (whether it's addressed to you directly or through your insurance company), how to find good financial deals and discounts and how to dispel the myth that living without health insurance is shameful, dangerous or indicative of not being worthy of the best care available.

So, I wrote a great little magazine article on the topic and touched lightly on each of several lessons I had learned. But there was so much more to it. The article was really just a drop in the bucket but I was happy with it and proud of it. I met with a literary agent who took a look at my notes for the cutesy chick-lit books I was hoping to work on and was unenthused, to say the least. While I had his ear, though, I felt compelled to show him some of my other work. He took one look at my healthcare article and declared, "Now there's your book!"

I was so excited to hear that something of mine (even if it was my husband's idea – and don't think he'll ever let me forget it!) was worthy of the literary world. I immediately started doing the research for this enormous project. As much as I have learned about healthcare I knew that there was so much more that I was yet unaware of. The first place I went was to the U.S. Census Bureau's web site to find out how many of you out there are like me, in regards to health insurance. I found that, according to the 2005 census, nearly 47 million people in the United States do not have health insurance, which equates to approximately 16 percent of our nation's population. What surprised me even more was the fact that a significant portion of these makes a good living. One common myth about people without health insurance is that they are living on or below the poverty line. According to that same census, of the 46.6 million Americans without health insurance, more than 17 million have a household income greater than $50,000 annually and of those nearly nine million earn more than $75,000 per year. That's a lot of people CHOOSING to live without health insurance. This certainly did not fit the stereotype I had in mind of the average family currently living without health insurance. I envisioned all of the other insuranceless families to be inner city dwellers of considerable poverty. My eyes are ever opened wider the more I delve into this topic that seems to have grabbed me by the shoulders and screamed, "Talk about me!"

The numbers continue to astound me. The majority of people in the United States who are not covered by health insurance are white, middle-aged, native-born Americans with a moderate income and living in the suburban south. And here all along I mistakenly thought that we were so different from the community around us in this respect.

This is why I wrote this book. The poor, yearning masses, the working class and the financially comfortable are all in the same boat.

Their reasons may be different but the result is the same – we are all fighting the same uphill battle for decent healthcare at affordable prices.

Nothing that I present to you in this book is a secret, but some of it may surprise you and hopefully all of it will interest, educate and improve you and your quality of healthcare.

The other reason I wrote this book is that, well, SOMEONE had to! All other books on healthcare deal with politics, social issues, medical jargon and can typically cure insomnia by page two. I'm hoping that I can supply interesting stories about my experiences, invaluable information based on what I've learned and present it in a friendly, interesting, easy-to-read format.

Why not?

So, why NOT have health insurance? As I said earlier, for us it started out as a financial decision – we just couldn't afford it. Since then, however, it has grown into a lifestyle choice.

Aside from the financials, my husband and I have always been independent thinkers and we just don't like being told what to do. Once the HMO plan was discarded we began to feel a certain sense of freedom in our healthcare choices. If we didn't like the way we were treated at one doctor's office we simply made an appointment with another. We didn't have to ask permission or get a written referral. Switching doctors was a snap and so was getting second opinions. I have always been a bit cynical about getting second opinions under the HMO scheme – it just seemed like there was no point to seeing a second doctor who had been referred to you by the first doctor. Chances are they're college or golf buddies or something of the sort. I felt like once they see which doctor you came from and reviewed the records that come with you they would just back each other up. When I get a second opinion, I want an unbiased, fresh opinion from someone unconcerned with covering for an old crony. I am much more comfortable with finding my own alternate opinions and am now free to do so.

When we first went HMO-less I always filled out the doctor's check-in paperwork with "none" in the insurance policy blanks but never thought to tell the doctor. I guess I was afraid they would treat me with less respect, condescendence, poor quality or worse yet – not at all. One of my doctors (most likely the only doctor who'd ever actually looked at the forms) piped up one day and asked me about our lack of insurance. A bit embarrassed I explained that my husband and I are self-employed and it just got too expensive for a family of four. Ever since then she has discounted her services for all of our appointments – and never has she treated me poorly or with contempt. After that I gained more confidence in our decision and have mentioned our lack of insurance to every doctor we've seen at the beginning of each appointment and found that most are willing to give a cash discount.

In not having health insurance I've become a much smarter caretaker for my family. I keep excellent records of doctor's visits, medical receipts and documentation, phone calls, and estimates. I also do more research – I Google every doctor before we make appointments and do background checks on them. I call around to get a feel for doctors and their staff as well as to get pricing ahead of any appointments I make. I check every medical bill that we get and question anything that is unexpected, confusing or just seems wrong. I negotiate everything. I was never this vigilant when we had an HMO. Why should I have been – that's what they're for, right? Since ditching the plan, I realize now how naïve that was because HMO's don't look out for your family the way you would. Not only that but when doctors send in bills the HMO will simply pay their agreed upon rate and bill you for the rest. At that point there's little for you to dispute with your doctor because the bill is long overdue and has become so confusing that even they don't often know what you're paying for.

In addition to these and numerous other reasons we continue to keep away from health plans, we have an overall sense of control over our medical destinies. We no longer have to wonder and worry, should catastrophe come our way, are we covered and for how much, what will the fallout costs be? Will the nearest hospital admit and treat us immediately without our referrals in place, etc. I have seen people pushed aside while awaiting treatment because their insurance companies have claimed they aren't in the right hospital or because they didn't call ahead for a referral. I would never want someone I love to go untreated for any number of minutes while waiting for an insurance company to respond.

What's more, everything is simpler, easier and less time consuming without an HMO to deal with. There's less paperwork to fill out, less loops in the billing system, etc. This is one of the reasons I'm so sure that doctors are forthcoming with discounts in their services to my family – they know that there's less hassle with the paperwork shuffle when they treat us and that they are going to get paid in full before I leave the office. $50 now and no more paperwork is better than billing $100 later and spending nearly that much money on hourly staff rates to get the insurance paperwork in order and track down the delayed payment.

How to Decide

It took a long, healthy period of consideration before we were comfortable with our decision to drop our HMO; there were several things we had to think about and look into first. One of the biggest obstacles to overcome is the mental and emotional barrier that keeps you with an HMO or other plan. Can we *mentally and emotionally* be without health insurance? It can seem really scary not having a plan in place, but ultimately it came down to this: without an insurance policy you just have to make alternate plans. It doesn't mean that you aren't prepared for medical crises. It doesn't mean that you aren't protecting your family. All it means is that you have other plans for your medical care. If your child breaks an arm and you aren't insured it doesn't mean you won't seek or find the treatment he or she needs or that you won't be able to afford the ambulance ride and hospital treatment. It just means that you are going to go about it a bit differently – especially the payment part.

I must admit when we first set out into the world of do-it yourself medical care I was a bit ashamed of our insuranceless status. I didn't want my mommy-friends to know or the preschool teachers, I was even embarrassed by the little N/A I had to write down in the insurance information box on our medical forms at the doctor's office. I felt like the receptionists were looking down, even sneering, at me. *Easy for them,* I thought to myself, *they probably get all the medical care in the world for free.* Not only was I embarrassed and ashamed for others to know our little family secret, I was terrified that one of my sons would have a terrible accident – boys will be boys, you know! Or that one of my seemingly healthy little cherubs would be suddenly diagnosed with some life threatening disease, leaving us destitute from the expenses, or worse – unable to convince a doctor to care for him because we didn't have an HMO to back us. I'm not sure where these fears came from but now that I look back on it I chalk it up to the fear of the unknown coupled with my extreme talent for always seeing the worst case scenario in any situation.

The longer we went without health insurance the more I realized that my fears were unfounded. Not only were my fears allayed, I found more and more ways of securing better, more affordable care. The number of alternatives is staggering. There are so many factors that most of us never know or think about when we are in the HMO rut. So much information is not relayed to us and so we just chug along doing what the insurance company and doctors tell us, not because it's wise or practical, but because it's all we know.

I liken it to grade school. We were sent and send our children there and it's a great way to get an education. But it isn't until we and our children step out into the real world that we truly get an education and we come to realize that what we learned in school is just a fraction of what can potentially be learned.

As with any fearful situation, the more you learn about what you fear the more comfortable you become with it.

I also got over my embarrassment of the situation. Despite the odd looks I still get when people find out I have no insurance, I am much more confident in stating it now. Where once I would reply meekly, "No, we don't have any.", blush and fade away, now I explain boldly, "No, we decided several years ago that we just didn't want it; it didn't make financial sense to us." Many people are very intrigued by this and love to ask questions about how it works and how we've managed all these years without it. The more I explain, the more intrigued they become and I can spot a sense of jealousy in many faces at the thought of the bravery, freedom and lessons we've experienced since taking the world by storm.

Just as important as how you *feel* about living without health insurance is how this decision will affect your finances. This is a tricky equation to figure out but it really is a matter of simple math to determine approximately how much money you would spend each year with and without insurance and compare the two.

The first step was gathering all of our medical receipts from the previous 12-month period, including doctor's visits, prescription and over-the-counter medications, insurance premiums, laboratory invoices and any other pertinent expenses. Then we added up everything that we'd paid out-of-pocket over the past 12 months.

The next step got a little tricky and involved calling doctors and our insurance company for information. What we were trying to determine is what our expenses *would have been* had we not been covered by insurance. First, we took out all of our insurance payments. What was left were the receipts, invoices and bills for our actual medical expenses. For our doctor's visits, instead of looking at what we'd paid for the co-payments, we had to look at what the actual bill total was and add that in. Then we did the same for our prescription medications and other receipts. Some of the invoices only showed our portion of the bill after insurance so we then had to ask the doctor, pharmacist or insurance company what the total bill was or would have been if the HMO hadn't been involved.

To give you an example of this type of comparison, here is what I found when I started "doing the math" to determine how viable our insurance was (keep in mind, my family expenses were very small at the time and that this was several years ago).

This is a look at what we actually paid for insurance, doctors' visit co-pays, medicine, etc.:

Insurance Premiums	$580 x 12 mos. = $6,960.00
Birth Control Pills	15 x 12 mos. = 180.00
Annual Physicals	20 x 4 people = 80.00
Dental Check-up/Cleaning	85 x 8 (2x/yr x 4 ppl) = 680.00
Other Dental Work	700.00
Miscellaneous Medications	50.00

Annual Total = $8,650.00

This is approximately what that same year looks like without insurance:

Birth Control Pills	$20 x 12 = $240.00
Annual Physicals	190 x 4 = 760.00
Dental Check-ups/Cleanings	85 x 8 = 680.00
Other Dental Work	700.00
Miscellaneous Medications	50.00

Annual Total = $2430.00

Keep in mind that this isn't exactly an "apples to apples" comparison. What you are looking at is what our current medical expenses would have been without our insurance chipping in. In reality, what we've found is that doctor's visits (and sometimes other medical expenses) will not be the same price without insurance. For example, we were previously paying a $20 co-payment on a $190 doctor visit. After we dropped our insurance, however, our doctor dropped her prices for us and now the same visit costs about $90. So, in effect, we have saved not only money from insurance premiums, but also $100 per doctor visit.

By our own methods and math, having insurance actually cost us $6,220.00 more for that particular year. This number astounded me. More than $6,000 annually wasted just for the sake of having insurance "just in case". I must admit that our family is very frugal when it comes to medical expenses. We're not one of those families who run to the doctor every time someone has a sniffle, sore throat or cough. We take very little medication, prescription or over-the-counter. Additionally, no one in my family has any medical conditions, allergies or predisposition to sickness and we had decided not to get pregnant again (another costly medical condition). As a result of these factors, having health insurance is mainly seen in my family as money down the drain. At the time of this discovery we really needed that extra money for other bills that we deemed more necessary. My husband and I agreed that the $6,620.00 we would save by cutting out health insurance would help us meet our other monthly obligations and that when things were a bit more steady, income-wise, we would set aside as much of that savings as possible into an investment so that if an emergency should arise we would have the cash on hand to deal with it without feeling devastated.

Just to give you a better sense of how things have progressed over time I've worked out our medical expenses of a more recent year. I've also put some notes in with the numbers as a partial explanation of the expense.

Monthly Birth Control Pills....$0 – My doctor gave me free samples she'd received from pharmaceutical companies.

Annual Physicals....$90 x 4 = **$360** – After discussing our double self-employment status and our lack of insurance, my doctor discounted our appointments.

Dental Cleanings, X-rays, Fillings, etc. ....**$2000** – Although this seems high, it would have been more because one of my sons needed a lot of dental work – teeth sealed, capped, pulled, spacers installed, etc. The dentist, however needed some brochures for a new business she'd started and so we bartered services for some of the dental work.

Oral Surgery....**$1180** – My other son had a cyst removed from under some impacted teeth. The original estimate was about $10,000! A second opinion was obtained and we were quoted $1400 for the same procedure, but the surgeon said that the operation went easier and more quickly than expected and so he gave us a further discount.

Miscellaneous Medications....**$20** – This, too, would have been much more except that we always remembered to ask for the generic medications on the $4 prescription list at Wal-Mart and Target.

Annual Total = $3,560.00

From this you can see that our medical expenses have increased slightly, but we are still not paying out-of-pocket anywhere near what we were when we had health insurance. In fact, we're still not paying even half of what we were responsible for under our HMO. I felt particularly good about our lack of insurance after this last year when we were faced with a semi-emergency; my son's oral surgery.

This past year really taught me so much. Until then I knew that we had made the right decision, in terms of health insurance, but we really hadn't been tested. I really still didn't know what would happen if something detrimental arose. There was still that nagging feeling in the back of my maternal mind that made me wonder if something devastating was around the corner how would we deal with it? Could we afford it? Would it break us? Now I know. I spent many sleepless nights wondering if we'd be better off having insurance and not worrying about the cost of surgery. Frankly, though, I think we would have been worse off. I would not have done the research, I would have taken the doctors at their word, I would not have had the deep sense of understanding that I have now about what my son was going through and what it meant and we would have taken for granted everything they wanted to do and let them. We would have cost the insurance company thousands of needless dollars for no reason.

It makes the kids feel better, too – they know they are well taken care of by smart parents who don't just let doctors do whatever they want. They see the pains taken by their parents who are on the Internet researching their problem, talking to friends about any past experiences they may have in that area. They get to see different doctors and tell you how each one made them feel and which one they like the best and they get a better understanding of how to best take care of themselves.

Not only did this experience help my son learn how loved he is by seeing the exceptional care that we took in getting him the best care, he also learned (on a deeper level that he probably won't be conscious of until he's an adult) how to take matters into your own hands, do the work, and take care of important things in a careful manner. Both lessons are extremely important. In a world where so many things are taken for granted, it's great to teach our children to be responsible and conscientious and that not everything in life will come easily or instantaneously.

There are still even more things to consider about health insurance. If you have an existing condition that causes you to visit doctors frequently or fill numerous prescription medications, you may spend a significant amount of money for these if you do not have health insurance.

I have a dear friend who suffers from Fibro Myalgia. For her, living without health insurance would be dire. For one thing, Fibro Myalgia is an umbrella diagnosis that really just says there's a bunch of little things wrong with you that, when combined, cause you a lot of pain and other negative conditions and side effects. While modern medicine hasn't yet developed a way to treat this disease by itself, doctors are busy treating patients with Fibro Myalgia one symptom at a time. My friend admitted to me that she sees three different specialists each month. That's almost one doctor's visit a week. Additionally, she pays out-of-pocket right now about $200 each month for her medications, which is just her share of the cost. Were she to take on these expenses in full she would be beyond broke. So, for her paying a few hundred dollars each month for health insurance actually saves her tens of thousands of dollars each year.

For her, I would never advise dumping her health insurance policy. What I would advocate, however, is doing a little research on her own to find out what new treatments and medications are available for Fibro Myalgia patients, if there are any clinical studies in her area that she might be able to become a part of, if there are any specials or deals out there for people with her ailment and any cheaper alternatives for the medications she's taking.

"I think it's better to have insurance," said the Administrative Director of a large treatment facility in northern Virginia, "not for the smaller, annual things but for the large issues like car accidents or cancer; even with reduced payment plans you could be stuck with tens of thousands of dollars in medical costs."

He did admit, however, that he's seen patients who's HMOs have dumped them after just a short period of treatment citing they'd maxed out their lifetime coverage.

If you do a cost analysis of your own medical expenses like I showed you with mine you will probably notice how expensive doctors' visits, treatments and prescriptions would be for you if you weren't covered by a health plan. A good idea in these cases may be to send an email or set up a telephone conference or consultation (look for whatever method will be at no cost) with your doctor. You will want to ask him or her what they would charge you for these visits if you are without insurance and make sure that they know that you are looking for a discounted rate and that without insurance their normal rates may be a hardship for you. Ask if you can set up a contract situation with a payment plan – for example, you could agree to four appointments per year for the sake of your condition at $120 dollars per visit and you agree to pay $40 dollars a month for the year. Also ask about the medications you are on. Are they completely necessary? Can the doctor provide free or discounted medications from their own supply closet? Can he or she prescribe a cheaper or generic version of the same medications to save you money?

Lastly, be sure to inquire as to possible complications from your condition. What other conditions can arise from your existing condition and what will that mean in terms of medical care and prescription medications? How can these side conditions be prevented?

Be sure, also, to do some research on your condition and the medications you are taking. Don't be afraid to delve in and find your own conclusions – finding out that your doctor is wrong or that he or she is not providing you with available alternatives is much better than letting things go and taking his word at face value just for the sake of not wanting to hurt his feelings.

Another consideration is the current and past health of your family. A great way to find out about the future health of your family is to find out about the past and present conditions of the people you are related to.

I suggest making a family project and get all the help you can find. This will be something like a family tree. Start off with a list of everyone in your immediate family, then add on the previous generation and keep adding as far back as anyone in your family can remember. Do not add anyone who does not share blood with you or your spouse. For example, your stepfather and your brother's wife need not be included in this project.

I would be remiss, however, if I didn't mention that this project can become quite depressing at times. My mother did a miniature version of the project I am proposing here and the document that she handed me was only one page long, but boy did it pack a punch. It was like watching a train wreck, I couldn't tear my eyes off that page, even though it was thoroughly dismal. Aside from the lucky few ancestors of my mother's who died instantly from a car wreck or freak biking accident, they were all taken after a lengthy fight with cancer in their 50s and 60s.

This does not bode well for a 30-ish white female American who has lived under the assumption that she has a good 50 to 60 years left. For a week I walked around in a funk -I was middle-aged at 30! I couldn't get past that fact. And then I realized, that wasn't a *fact*, but only a warning, a set of probabilities, a challenge, knowledge and a much needed kick in the pants to live life to the fullest and to take better care of myself. The key is that even if what you find is disheartening, it's vital knowledge. Your findings are your own road map to your future health, you will now know what it is you are battling against. Although there is no sure link between any particular facet of life and the onset of cancer, we do know that certain things can decrease one's chances of contracting the disease. So, instead of dwelling on the fact that I have about a 50 percent chance of dying in my early AARP years (my father's side of the family, with only a few exceptions, all died in their 80s and 90s of old age), I prefer to spend my time appreciating the vitality of my life now and improving it for myself and my children so that perhaps I can beat the odds.

You can do this project in several different manners. I, for one, am big on Excel spreadsheets, but this could also be a handwritten chart or any other method that makes sense to you. For column headers (back to the spreadsheet idea) I would have "Name", "Relation", "Date of Birth", "Date of Death" (if it applies), "Overweight: Yes/No", "Smoker: Yes/No", "Cause of Death" and "Known Medical Conditions". Then just fill in the spreadsheet with all of the data you can collect.

This might also be another point at which you consult your doctor – I would include this discussion in your regular annual physical. I would bring your organized findings to your appointment and have the doctor look them over (if possible, bring a copy that the doctor can keep in your file). Then ask her what your family's history means to you and your future – what should you be concerned about, what should you not be concerned about, how can you better care for yourself and prevent the concerning factors?

The overall health of yourself and your family today as well as risk factors for your future may help you determine if you can live without health insurance practically. You may find that, knock on wood, you are all healthy and destined to live long and healthy lives. You may find that you should be concerned with obesity and diabetes in your retirement years. You could find that there are some concerns with cancer at middle age. Take all of these factors into consideration when deciding on your health insurance status.

The best way to find out about living without health insurance is to talk to people who have done it or are currently doing it. I have met people who have been in terrible automobile accidents and who needed long term hospitalization, rehabilitation and medication who found out, the hard way, that their insurance company just stopped covering them after so many weeks or months. In many cases your insuran has a maximum payout for each member of your family per . lifetime. By the time you hit this ceiling, you are essentially wi. insurance for the remainder of the year, or possibly for the rest of your lifetime. Although the HMO may have paid a portion of this new large debt incurred by an accident, you are stuck with paying the remainder of your medical costs on your own at the rate the HMO negotiated with the doctors and hospitals. Had you been on your own from the start, you could have negotiated with the doctors and hospitals on your own behalf and perhaps made a better deal and set up a payment plan that would benefit all of the parties involved.

Please keep in mind that I have not personally been through every type of medical situation. I bring up some of these situations, hypothetical and otherwise, to make you think about your situation and the future health of your family with regard to health insurance. I see so many commercials and ads for health insurance companies, health organizations and prescription clubs and they all attempt to make us feel like living without a plan or a club or a card or a membership is such a dire thing. That to operate in the world of healthcare we are helpless on our own, that we couldn't possibly find our own way, that we are failures or daredevils if we fail to join the masses who already have coverage. The truth of the matter is that they are just trying to make money – it's what all businesses are set up to do, nothing more and nothing less. Its like those toy commercials you see during the holidays, they inundate our children by the hundreds. They are the coolest, hippest, neatest stuff in the world and you must have one or you're no one. And the kids lap it up, they beg and beg for these things for Christmas, Kwanzaa and Chanukah. But, as parents, we have grown wise to the advertising bug – we try to reason with our children that these things they see on the television are not necessities and may not even be cool or fun at all in person. We are immune to commercial advertising, or so we think, until an ad for insurance comes on. Don't let them do the thinking for you anymore. Do the research, find the facts, discover the truth and make your own decisions for yourself. I will never say that having health insurance is wrong or bad, I just know that it isn't the right decision for my family. It may or may not be necessary for you and your family, but at least consider all the facts and make an informed and educated decision based on something real.

Finally, I would like to discuss the long-term effects of having a health insurance policy. Even for those of you who have done the cost analysis and have determined that having health insurance is financially advantageous to you, have you really considered the cost of doing business in this manner for decades? It's easy to look at the small picture. You see what your medical expenses add up to in a 12-month period and you can see what it is you pay for your insurance, your outofpocket expenses and such, but try to see the big picture, too.

There are two big pictures, as I see it. First is your big picture and the second is the national or global big picture. For your own big picture I suggest reading the fine print of your insurance policy. What are the maximums that you are covered for? If you contract a debilitating disease or illness, how long will your insurance cover your medical expenses or up to what amount? What are the negotiated rates that your insurance company has set up with your healthcare provider and are they actually less than what you would pay if you had an appointment without insurance? What freedom do you have to negotiate your medical fees when your insurance company already has a set rate plan established with your doctors, hospitals and pharmacies?

Even after several years of living without health insurance I still wonder if someday I will be faced with a medical tragedy in my family and mounting medical expenses that neither I nor my children will be able to pay off in our lifetimes. The truth of the matter is that insurance or not, we are all equally likely to face this scenario. I have heard numerous stories of average people, with health insurance, who have decided to file bankruptcy as their only solution to the hundreds of thousands or more in medical expenses that they were left with after suffering through long illnesses and medical treatments with loved ones.

I also know of one couple who had a lesser, but similar experience. The daughter and son-in-law of some friends of ours were buried under a heavy load of medical expenses -a combination of health insurance premiums owed to their HMO and their out-of-pocket portions owed to doctors, physical therapists and the hospital. The load of these expenses wiped them out. They were left with nothing to pay their mortgage or utility bills with and eventually their home was foreclosed on. Their insurance company and medical expenses left them, literally, homeless.

The lesson here: insurance companies are not in business to help you, they are in the business of making money -just like all businesses. They are not non-profit organizations -they are only in existence to make money. That is why they all have pages of fine print included in their policies; they have bailout clauses for nearly every possible scenario. Why? Because they want to ensure that they don't lose money, they don't want to cover your thousands of dollars in medical bills every year for hundreds of dollars in return. It's only worth it to them to cover your medical expenses if the fees they get in return are larger than their outlay. What you're really paying for is the benefit of paying in a little bit on a monthly basis so that you, hopefully, won't have to pay a large sum all at once in a medical emergency. The only other benefit to HMOs is, supposedly, their negotiated doctor's fees, which in theory should be lower than normal due to the large volume of visits, treatments, etc. that they handle every day. It's sort of like shopping at

Costco, the prices are lower, again supposedly, because you are buying through a volume plan.

The problem is that you may actually be able to negotiate better on a one-on-one basis with your individual healthcare providers to lower your expenses and you may be better served by saving your monthly premiums and investing them into something strong and steady so that you have a larger lump sum of cash should a medical emergency arise.

As far as the national or global big picture is concerned, try to think about how your medical plan affects the world around you. It's hard to do when you're just looking at your premiums and your own bottom line, but if you really think about it health insurance is a very large problem in our nation -one we all complain about yet go on day-to-day living the same way. Maybe if we have a better understanding of how health insurance works, we can change it so that it actually does work for us.

First of all, as I said, insurance companies are only in business to make money. They won't go out of their way to help you but if they can help you in the process of making money then they're okay with that, so don't expect them to bend over backwards. Your doctor, on the other hand, is a much more conscientious business person. Doctors, first and foremost, are part of your community; they are in touch with the issues going on in your area, the lifestyles and income potentials of the local area and have gone into the medical profession mostly out of a dedication to help people. It goes without saying that if you want to appeal to someone's humanitarian side when negotiating your medical costs, you will have a much better chance face-to-face with your local doctor than in a phone call to a large corporation.

As for the HMO's negotiated price list, it isn't always a better deal. Let's say your HMO has negotiated with your doctor that an annual checkup appointment is worth $125, the urine test is worth $35 and blood work costs $50. If you have all of these services provided for you at your next visit, your bill will be a total of $210. You don't care, you have a co-pay of $20, the HMO is responsible for the other $190 anyway so you think nothing of it. The problem with this is that in Los Angeles the regular fees for these services may have totaled $300 before the HMO negotiated fees, but in your small town USA your doctor was only charging $150 before the HMO butted in with their list. So now, when you look at it, your HMO really raised the prices in your neighborhood and is overpaying for your medical expenses. Not only are they overpaying, but they are causing doctors to raise their rates, making it more difficult for those of us without insurance, they are also paying out more than they should, which they will evaluate next quarter or next year and raise your premiums. It's a vicious cycle and it keeps escalating ever upward. People with insurance are finding it harder and harder to keep up with their premiums because as they go up employers are less willing to supplement them to the extent at which they are currently and individuals are becoming increasingly unable to pay their own premiums since incomes are not rising at the same rates as insurance plans.

Want to find out how your insurance company has really helped you out? Call up your doctor, anonymously, and tell them you are an uninsured individual considering switching medical practices and are wondering what they charge for a routine physical. Then call up your insurance company and ask them what their negotiated fee is for a routine physical. Should be an interesting experiment.

Chapter 2: Uncertainty be Darned
We Really Did it?

After going through all of the paperwork and analysis that I mentioned in Chapter 1 we knew, unequivocally, that health insurance was something we could, or should, depending on how you look at it, live without. What a very startling realization.

For many people, living without health insurance is a major emotional hurdle. It was for me as well. When my family decided to cut out the monthly expense of health insurance I was fiercely afraid. Here I was, mother of two young boys and wife to a self-employed contractor: three people who typically spend each and every day defying gravity and the odds of getting hurt. As a parent you tend to hear horror stories of terrible ways in which spouses and children become involved in medical emergencies. Then, of course, there's the looming sense that Mother Nature is hovering over you waiting to throw you a curveball in the form of some unforeseen illness. The thought of being without health insurance can be more than just unsettling; it can be unnerving and downright paralyzing.

It might feel this way to you, too, especially if you're a woman. While that statement might seem sexist, women are, generally speaking, more emotional as well as the naturally-elected caregivers of the family.

"The health of every person's life who is significant to a woman is important to her," said Nancy Dailey, Ph.D., sociologist and award-winning author. "Healthcare is a cost on many levels for a woman: it's not just about caring for family when they're sick, it's socially decided that the woman will give care to their spouses, children, siblings and parents in aspects of medical care, custody, financial responsibility and psychological and emotional support."

That's a mighty large undertaking and one that women tend to step into without much forethought. We truly want to take on these roles and help make everyone better and ensure they receive the best care. Unfortunately that also impedes the ability for the main caregiver (whether female or male) to obtain and retain a quality job with steady pay. It also can take a toll on that person's own emotional and sometimes physical health.

Whether the main caregiver will admit it or not, being responsible for everyone's well-being is a huge burden, one that becomes even heavier when there's no health insurance policy in place. Having no health insurance means having even more responsibilities and giving even more time to ensuring proper care is given to your loved ones. It's a situation that must be weighed very carefully if you have the decision to make. For some, obviously, having health insurance just isn't an option, but for those, like my family, who have it (either through employers or on their own) and are considering doing without, it's a decision that should not be taken lightly or made on the spur of the moment.

I took a leap of faith, though not without a lot of careful consideration. I decided to believe my husband when he said it would be okay. He was right, but I was skeptical at the time. Although I had no assurances -no one ever does when it comes to the health of your family -I came to the realization that I could literally think and worry about it forever and sit on the fence for all eternity, or I could jump on board with my husband and give it a try. Fear is a very big thing to overcome. The thing about fear is that you'll never get past it unless you face it head-on.

It turns out my husband was right -everything has been okay. I won't tell you that we haven't had any health concerns in the family since cancelling our health insurance policy, but I can tell you that the four of us have been well taken care of and every incidence of illness and medical attention needed was met and dealt with responsibly and well. As it turns out, we've become aware that, for us, health insurance was nothing more than a needless monthly expense. It was not an asset, it was not a service and it did not serve us well. In fact, it was more of a hindrance to us, draining us each month for very little in return.

Many people aren't as daring as my husband and myself and are not used to living "outside the box" the way we're accustomed to. I attribute this to the fact that we are a dual-self-employment family, meaning that we've pretty much had to come up with creative living in many ways. We are square pegs by comparison to the majority of mainstream America. We don't fit into loan packages, we don't always pay our bills on time or in their entirety all at once, we don't get steady paychecks and generally find our year broken up into, not pay periods, but phases of feast or famine -times where we have an abundance of cash on hand and others where scraping together enough money to order a Big Mac would be an impossibility. What I am trying to say is that for us, living differently than the perceived norm is actually normal for us. For families who try to live by the perceived norm, living without health insurance is a horrifying thought. Fortunately, it doesn't have to be a horrifying reality.

The biggest deal, truly, is getting over it mentally. People have told us that we are crazy to live without health insurance. They've told us horror stories (usually not firsthand accounts, though, just rumors, I've noticed) and have even tried to make us feel ashamed of not having insurance. The truth is, though, millions of Americans are currently living without health insurance and many of them do so by choice and are not ashamed, they don't feel sorry for themselves and they don't think they would be better off if they had insurance. Sometimes things become so common in this nation that people follow the herd for so long that they forget to really think about it. We took the time to really look over the situation and the truth of the matter was/is, for us, that health insurance was just a perceived need and the fear of not having it was quickly outweighed by our real need to keep our family afloat with more pressing expenses. We've never been concerned with what other's think about the way we do things nor worried about "keeping up with the Jones'" and the way they do things. We knew this was right for us and scary or not, we needed to try to make it work.

Remember your mother's words, "If everyone else jumped off the Brooklyn Bridge, would you do it, too?" We tried to put health insurance into that perspective. While jumping off the bridge may seem like a good idea to others, is it really the right decision for us? Health insurance is really one of those things you need to think about with regard to your own well-being. Just because you think everyone else has it and the healthcare industry tells you you should have it, doesn't make it true.

I've found that there are ways we could have done it differently if we weren't prepared to take such a big step right off the bat. There are a few safety nets available had we really felt that we could benefit by cancelling our insurance policy but were too scared to follow through. There is such a thing as catastrophic health insurance (also known as high deductible health insurance or major medical insurance). The premiums are much smaller than regular health insurance plans, but they don't cover routine visits or treatments, only very high cost care including hospital stays, major surgery, etc.. This means that we would be living day-to-day without health insurance but should disaster strike, we would have insurance to fall back on.

A 2008 article I found about catastrophic insurance on insurance.com stated that "the monthly premium for a 21-year old, nonsmoking female to be $29." Catastrophic health insurance works just like regular health insurance but you pay out of pocket up to a much higher level before coverage applies, and because of this their lifetime coverage can be much more than regular insurance. The same article noted that deductibles tend to start around $500 or more and, like most other types of insurance, the higher you set your deductible, the lower your premiums are. You have to be careful though to set realistic deductibles for yourself -while it's tempting to set the deductible at, say, $15,000 so that your premium is next to nothing, keep in mind that if you have surgery that costs $15,000 or more, you are personally responsible for that first $15,000 out-of-pocket, which may be difficult to come up with, especially if that surgery keeps you from returning to work right away.

Catastrophic health insurance is a nice, inexpensive safety net to have, but it is one more payment to keep up with, so we didn't consider it seriously at that time. It's nice to know it's out there though....just in case....maybe someday.

Other safety nets out there come in the form of state or local children's insurance policies. Many of these organizations offer free or inexpensive health coverage for dependent children. Where I live, there is a state-developed healthcare program for children and pregnant mothers in the Commonwealth of Virginia who are not currently covered by a health insurance policy and who meet maximum income requirements. I believe that nearly all states have some sort of program like this, it's basically MedicAid.

The program, which is run by the state, is called FAMIS (Family Access to Medical Insurance Security). The insurance is free to eligible families -there are no membership fees or monthly premiums the only fees you may encounter are co-payments of $2 or $5 for certain services. Eligibility is dependent on residency and income caps; a family of four is currently eligible if they earn no more than $42,400 per year. The program covers things like doctor visits, well-baby checkups, hospital visits, vaccinations, prescription medicine, tests and X-rays, dental care, emergency care, vision care and mental health care.

I must admit, these programs are new to me, just discovered in the course of doing research for this book. I was intrigued, indeed. Now, due to the economic crisis that has hit our nation so hard recently my silver lining (if you can really consider it so) is that my family now qualifies for FAMIS and my boys can get free healthcare from the state, so I started digging a bit deeper. Although we're perfectly happy with our current health plan of the DIY variety, I'm a sucker for anything that claims to be *free* despite my best efforts to be cynical and believe that there is *no free lunch*.

So I filled out the on-line application for my children. Upon completing it -and it was quite lengthy -I was asked to print out the confirmation form, sign it and send it in with some tax forms and proof of income. I mailed all of that in and awaited the results. While I'd be happy to have health insurance for the kids -especially the dental plan bit -I was still skeptical. When I looked through the directories of doctors in my area who accept these plans none of our current physicians and dentists are among them, save the saintly second-opinion oral surgeon my son saw last year. When I called my doctor to see if they would accept this plan they said that they would not and that it was basically a Medicaid plan. I guess they feel that having to deal with billing through the government is even less beneficial than dealing with HMOs. Which begs the question: which practices ARE willing to do this and what type of care will you get from them?

I am certain that there are decent doctors accepting these state-run medical plans, but they seem to be few and far between, and not in very convenient locations from my home. My general opinion is that if you don't mind switching doctors and you can find a great one who accepts these plans, it's a good deal -your children are covered with little to no money out of your own pocket and your own medical bills will be covered should you become pregnant. But still, I would be very careful in selecting your provider and keep an eye on the costs you're not paying. Essentially, I would advise continuing your vigilant stance on your family's healthcare as if you were still insuranceless.

As it turned out -it was a three month process to complete my children's FAMIS application process. I was a bit disappointed in the length of time it took and perhaps this isn't the norm -could be due to that pesky double-self-employment status I told you about earlier, but it was a bit frustrating. Essentially I applied for insurance for my boys mid-July and received confirmation that everything was in and good and ready for use the first week in October. Now, frustrations aside, I'm glad that I've done this. We'll have to see a new doctor and dentist this year, but I'm sure I can find good and qualified people, but if I don't like them, we can always just revert back to our own -no harm, no foul, and best of all -no money spent! And since the past year has been especially trying on our finances I like knowing that their dental cleanings, teeth sealants, annual physicals and timely vaccinations will cost me only a maximum of $5 per appointment between now and next summer (when I start the application process all over again.....sigh.)

After having this free state medical plan for my boys for a few months I realized -I really should take advantage of free medical care while we still have it (I guess I'm more optimistic than I give myself credit for -I'm counting on making more money next year). Anyway, I shopped the FAMIS directory and selected a pediatric dentist not too far away and a pediatric physician somewhat close to home (both are about 15 miles away -not too bad). We visited the dentist first.

My older son was immediately not thrilled when we pulled into the parking lot and got out of the car.

"Mom", he began to whine, "it looks like a place for really little k......"

And before he could finish the sentence he flung the door open and ran inside, face and palms pressed against the enormous fish tank in the center of the room.

"Oh, wow -look Mom! They've got fish."

And just like that, he was hooked. His brother and I took a little more convincing -of course we're not obsessed with marine life like my future Marine Biologist. Both kids had their routine check ups, X-rays, cleanings, etc. Which was great, because normally my older son can't bite the silly cardboard films the dentist puts in his mouth but it all went smoothly.

While we were there they discovered a cavity in each mouth and took care of it on the spot -no follow-up appointment necessary. This is where they really started to reel me in as well. Normally, with the dentists we've encountered, when we go for routine cleanings and check-ups anything else the dentist finds that she'd like to do means making another appointment. I'd always wondered if it was so they could charge more for a second time slot. I think I have my answer now. While the fillings were going in, I asked about sealants on the adult teeth to make sure they didn't get cavities on their "keepers", so they went ahead and sealed a few teeth, too. I never would have thought it possible -but I really like having this health plan for the boys. It was the first time ever that I've been in a dentist office completely relaxed. I didn't have to think about costs at all. I didn't have to wonder if they were trying to fool me or if I would have to sell a kidney to pay for what just happened.

In one afternoon both of my children had their teeth cleaned, a semi-annual check-up, X-rays taken, cavities filled and adult teeth sealed. The receptionist even made sure I had copies of all of the paperwork showing what they had done and how much they would be billing the state for me before I left. And it didn't cost me a cent.

Even better was that when she showed me what my services had cost, it really wasn't that bad, considering all that we'd had done. If (God willing) there comes a day when our high levels of income get us kicked off this wonderful plan, I know I'll be staying with this particular dental practice. By the time we left -we were all hooked! I think it's the first time we've all been to the dentist together and NO ONE left in tears.

As spring made it's way to Virginia, I realized that it had been two years since I'd taken the boys to get their annual physical. I felt very guilty about this, but they're very healthy and no one needed any vaccinations and with money so tight, we just didn't get there. This would be the year, I promised myself. Once I found the doctor we'd see, we set up the appointment. It was a large, new, somewhat chilly place - normally I don't like those. I prefer small, dim and cozy, but I tried to keep an open mind.

As I stood at the counter getting all of my son's paperwork in order, I saw an old friend of mine. I was shocked. This particular friend had moved to a town an hour away from us last year and she had driven all the way back just to see this doctor? We didn't get much time to talk, so I emailed her later and pumped her for all the info she could spare about this practice we'd chosen. Apparently she loves her son's doctor so much that, yes, she drives an hour into our town to see this man anytime any of her four children need medical care. Now that's an endorsement!

I can't say my boys and I got quite the same feeling, but the women behind the counter were a riot -a very friendly group of fun-loving people and the doctor was good. Perhaps it'll grow on us, but we certainly can't complain. Again, two annual check-ups later and we hadn't spent one dime. My older son even needed two shots that are required before heading off to middle school this fall.

That big kid, God love him, is SO⌐
He woke up one morning (this was before ·
his face completely swollen and eyes nearly
just to look at him. He kept telling me it really
but I just couldn't bear it so I took him to our nc
could relieve him (or me) any. Within an hour he'ᴄ
dismissed, sent to the pharmacy and we had liquid reliє.
was happy about that. The doctor's appointment dɪᴄ
anything, and neither did the medication.

It's been a really confusing time for me, what with all oɪ
medical care. I'm starting to doubt my belief system. Not really, buᴛ
battling with doctors and healthcare professionals for so long abo.
treatments and costs, it's just baffling to me to have the state take over
and make my life easier. It really is amazing. I've kept my vigilant watch
to make sure my boys are truly getting proper care, but it's just so nice to
be able to leave the doctor's office feeling lighter and relieved instead of
feeling better about the boys' health but worse about our budget.

I have to admit, having and enjoying a free state-run medical
plan for my children has thrown me for a loop. I never thought I'd be one
of those people taking handouts from the government. But I've given it a
lot of thought. My husband and I have worked very hard for many years.
We've lived and worked in this state for more than 20 years each and
we've definitely paid our fair share of taxes in to the state and federal
government. So why shouldn't they help take care of our children (and
us, financially, in the process) while we're having financial difficulties?

As much as I hate to admit it, they're doing a darn fine job of it,
too. And it's not as if we now strive to live below our state-defined
poverty level of $42,000 a year in income. Believe you me, when the
time comes that our businesses (and the economy) are doing better,
we'll gladly pull our children off of the FAMIS healthcare plan, but in
the meantime, this is a really great program and it's already helping us a
great deal. I highly recommend taking advantage of state and federal
assistance programs -If you truly need them. That's what they're there
for. And when you don't truly need them, then it's time to wean
yourself to make room for others facing hardships.

At any rate, if you're a resident of Virginia and you wish to see
if you qualify for FAMIS go to www.famis.org, or call 1-86687FAMIS.
To see if there's a comparable program in your state check out
www.insurekidsnow.gov, or call 1-877-KIDSNOW. Insure Kids Now
is a national campaign to offer affordable means by which our children
can receive excellent medical care without breaking the parents.

As for my husband and I; we are still living without health
insurance and managing our own care. Fortunately, we don't require
much in the way of care. I try to remember my well-woman exam every year
and my husband is a chronic believer in the "if it ain't broke, don't go

doctor" philosophy.

So, admittedly, that first step in cancelling our health insurance
y was a doozy for me emotionally, but I've come a long way since
ı. In about seven years I've gone from a paranoid worried mess to a
ıfident and competent family health provider. It amazes me how our
ecision-making process has changed where our healthcare is concerned
since we decided to be responsible for our own healthcare.
We've all grown and become much more cautious, vigilant and
conservative with respects to our family's care. It really is a growth
process, one I'm glad we've journeyed down. I have no qualms about
living without health insurance now. Finances are still something I
worry about from time to time, but if there's one thing heading down this
path has taught me it's that things tend to work out. Sometimes money is
tight and sometimes it's not an issue, but our health is important, so we
do whatever it takes to make sure it's well taken care of. What still
amazes me, however, is that we are much better at finding better care now
that we don't have insurance. When it's all up to you to figure out what
happens next, you tend to tread much more carefully and the result is
something you can be very proud of.

Chapter 3: All Insuranced Out
and No Place to Go

When we first dumped our insurance plan, we were free to see any doctor in the world without getting special permission or worrying about whether he or she is listed in a catalog of health care professionals. It's total freedom – but the number of choices can be overwhelming.

In just my little county – population 66,000 and growing – the skimpy community phone book lists over 140 businesses in the healthcare profession. That's a lot of doctors to choose from. I don't know about you, but I have trouble just making the choice of what to cook for dinner – and I'm talking chicken, hamburger or pork chops? How can you possibly figure out which practice is right for you out of 140?

I won't sugar coat it, it is a painstaking, time-consuming series of investigations and sometimes a bit of trial and error, but it's well worth the time investment. Having the right doctor means finding someone you really trust, not having a doctor who's diagnoses you question or doubt (although swear you will always, ALWAYS get a second opinion when it counts). You want someone who seems to genuinely care about how you and your family feel, someone who makes your children feel comfortable and who gives you choices and options when it comes to the care of the people you love.

After we ditched our last HMO, we reverted back to seeing the same family practitioner that we'd had under a previous insurance policy. I loved this doctor. He'd been my doctor since my parents first moved us to Virginia when I was twelve years old (just a *few* years ago -wink!). He'd known me all through my teen years, college, marriage and then became both of my boys' primary care physician and he was just the nicest guy, most competent doctor and even had his wife as a practice partner. How's that for family values?

Little by little though, the turnover rate in his office became astounding and before I knew it all of the capable nurses and staff members were gone, replaced only by inexperienced, incapable, and frankly uncaring people. As much as I loved my doctor, I loathed the rest of his staff. And every time we went to his practice we spent an hour or more there but only five minutes or less with him -the rest of the time we were in **their** hands and I was very uncomfortable with that.

To top it off, after a while they started declaring it their "policy" to get non-insured patients to pay a $100 cash deposit prior to seeing the doctor. This I found absurd and a bit offensive. After over a decade of being a patient there, they could no longer trust me to pay before leaving that day? The first time I had an appointment and was faced with this new policy I didn't have any cash on hand, so the receptionist told me I could just write her a check. While I expected to have to pay for my appointment before leaving, paying in advance was something I was skeptical about doing. Nonetheless, I asked her what the actual cost of my appointment would be. She said she had no idea and I argued with her that it would be silly for me to write a check for $100 in advance and then have to write another check at the end for the correct amount and wouldn't it make more sense just to write one proper check at the end of the appointment? She didn't care, all she knew was that if she didn't get $100 from me in one form or another right then and there I wasn't going to see the doctor. I was more than a little incensed but I acquiesced and wrote the $100 check.

The last straw was the day I brought both boys in to have their vaccinations that were due. Keep in mind that since they are a year and a half apart in age they needed different vaccinations. The nurse took the boys' height, weight, blood pressure, etc. and got their shots ready then exclaimed, "Whoops! I put all of one child's information in the other one's folder."

You know what that said to me? That she was also about to give one child's shots to the other child. Not good. Not good at all. It goes without saying that we have never been back. I hated leaving my trusty old doctor, but I just didn't trust his staff and my children's well-being is far more important to me than liking my doctor. So, we now had no insurance and no doctor. It was time to start doing some homework.

My first step in making any large decision is always the same – I run it up the flagpole! My husband always likens me and my girlfriends to a bunch of clucking hens but the truth of the matter is that they are my best source of information on any subject. I believe this is true of any group of friends. We all choose our friends based on the people surrounding us that we have the most in common with. It makes sense that when we need help making decisions, chances are our friends will have some sort of input – positive or negative. I never discount the negative stuff – it can be just as helpful as the positive. For example, Susan says she absolutely loves her Dr. Smith, he can see her on a moment's notice and doesn't scare the kids. Deb, on the other hand, says Dr. Smith is great but his nurse, Karen, is a bit of a crab.

So, I talked to everyone I know and asked them who their doctor is and if they would recommend them. I also found it interesting to find out who their previous doctor was and why they left – this can provide great insight. Maybe their last doctor was the best thing since sliced bread but they had to leave because of a change in insurance plans or maybe he was terrible and now you have one more out of your original 140 to cross off.

Not all of my polling was girl gab. I also sent an email blast – asking local people I don't see on a regular basis about their doctors. It's great because you can reach so many people all at once and as you get your replies back you can cross doctors off your list or put little stars next to the ones who were recommended. If I didn't have email I just would have had to do it the old-fashioned way – by phone or in person. I didn't want to make this a lifelong search, though, so I tried to keep it simple and direct and not over-think it – if a friend said something bad about a doctor, I didn't evaluate it or wonder if I could live with whatever it was they disliked – I just crossed them off the list, there were plenty of others to choose from.

From the list of remaining doctors I made a top three selection of the ones I would most likely choose from. I considered what others said about them, their office location/convenience, how many doctors were in their practice and started calling each of these doctors' offices and talking to the receptionist. My first question with a new practice is always, "Are you accepting new patients?" – there's no sense wasting your time in considering someone who isn't. Next I like to ask if the doctor is male or female – this may seem silly, but you can't tell if the phone book listing just says Dr. Soandso or if they have an ambiguous or foreign first name. Then I continue with a few random questions like how long the doctor has been practicing medicine and where they earned their highest degree. Some of this information isn't all that important, but it helps me determine the type of business the doctor is running. If this is a doctor you can trust your health with they should have a) a staff that doesn't mind answering the questions of potential patients, b) a staff that is capable of answering such questions and c) credentials that are worthy – Harvard and Princeton are great but what if their degree is from some third world country – how much confidence does that instill?

My next step would/should have been to use my computer to do a background check on the doctor. This is something that I've only recently learned about, but is something that I always do now. I would recommend this to anyone, regardless of insurance or location or length of time you've known your doctor. The second I learned how to do this for free, I immediately checked up on every doctor I'd ever seen.

If you don't have a computer or Internet access, get yourself to the public library or a friend's house. Web sites are always changing, but a Google search under "state health agencies" will typically give you a few pages that have a list, by state, of federally run organizations in order alphabetically by state. Click on your state and look over your state's health department site for something like "license lookup" or "doctor profiles" or "licensing and certification" or "licensure verification" – you get the idea. What you are looking for is a valid U.S. license to practice medicine for the doctor you are considering. (See appendix A for a state by state listing of health departments and web sites that contain license lookups or doctor profiles.)

The license verification or doctor profile should also tell you where that doctor practices, what his or her specialty is, how long they've held a valid license, when that license expires (not important unless it was last year and they haven't renewed it!). One of the most important things this background check provides is whether or not this doctor has any complaints or actions out against them. Dr. Soandso may be the nicest, most caring doctor in the universe but if he's about to be fined or have his license revoked because of malpractice or sexual harassment, then you need to know now before you give him or her any further consideration.

Another great source for finding public data in your state and about the doctors in your area is through www.fsmb.org/directory_smb.html. This is the web site of the Federation of State Medical Boards and each listing provides the available contact information for each board, including a web site link, where applicable. They claim that "The FSMB Physician Profile provides users with professional information on physicians and physician assistants licensed in the United States, and includes information on disciplinary sanctions, education, medical specialty, licensure history and locations."

You can search for dental healthcare professionals who are licensed through the American Dental Association at www.ada.org. From their home page, under the "Dental Professionals" column, click on "Member Directory". You will have to read and accept the terms of their site usage and then type in the parameters of your search, i.e. what service you are looking for and what city and state you desire. The site will only give you their contact information and state whether or not they are active ADA members, but at least you will know they are properly licensed.

To find out a little more about a dentist or other dental professional you can go to www.healthguideusa.org/state_dental_boards.htm and click on your state. For my state, Virginia, I went to License Lookup and typed in my son's oral surgeon's name and Zip Code where he practices and it came up with his name and contact information. When I click on his name it gives me his profile including his license number, issue and expiration date and says whether or not there is any additional public information available on his practice. In this case that category says "No", which I'm assuming is a good thing because according to their site "'Yes" means that there is information the Department must make available to the public pursuant to §54.1-2400.2.F of the Code of Virginia. For additional information click on the "Yes" link above. "No" means no documents are available. Sounds to me like a "Yes" means that there may be disciplinary records or complaints against the doctor.

At www.nabp.net, the National Association of Boards of Pharmacy provides a list of boards of pharmacy that are, again, listed by state. Each listing has the name of the executive director of the state board and all of the board's contact information including a web link and email address where possible. Again, on the Virginia board site you can click on License Lookup and find information on any specific pharmacy or pharmacist if you have their name and location. In order to find a licensed pharmacist, if you don't have someone particular in mind, select Pharmacist in the Occupation blank, select your state and type in the Zip Code where you are or where you will want to go to have prescriptions filled and a list of possibilities should pop up. The only problem I find with this site is that pharmacists often don't have their own business, they typically are located inside a big name department store, drug store or grocery store and this site only supplies the name and city/state where they are licensed and not the exact location where they can be found.

If you have trouble finding any of the state boards for your location just go to www.clearhq.org/boards.htm. The Council on Licensure, Enforcement and Regulation (CLEAR) has a complete repertoire of boards listed by location. You can click on Canada, United States or Professions and Occupations and find a listing for whatever board you seek. It also has a place where you can send them links if you find something on the Internet that they don't have a link to so that others may find it more easily.

All of these resources are fantastic and easy to use. I cannot stress enough how important it is to use these tools before allowing any healthcare professional to do ANYTHING to you or someone you love. Just so you know – it's never too late to do this. As soon as I found out about this little investigative tool, I immediately did a search on every doctor and dentist my family had been to in the past five years. Fortunately, I was very pleased at what I discovered – there was only one strike out against one of the health care professionals we were seeing and it turned out to be very silly, but I'm still glad I know. As it turns out our dentist was being fined – I was really scared, especially since we had just switched to her and we really, really love her. Luckily, I was able to pull up the disciplinary action report from her profile and found out that her big crime was claiming she was "the best" in the community in one of her ads and she got fined for her vanity -apparently arrogance is a punishable offense in the world of healthcare marketing. I can live with that! No mouths were hurt in that scandal so we decided to keep her.

Ok, so we polled, cold-called and investigated. Just call me Geraldo! And I was able to find a practice I was sure we would love. But there was still more to do. What I like to do next is something my mother warned me to never do – but, hey, it works, so I say go for it – judge a book by its cover! I like to drive around and take a look at the type of office space a practice is in, the neighborhood it's located in, etc. I do not like those large, pretentious, we-bilk-millions-each-year-from-our-patients-and-their-HMOs buildings. They immediately turn me off and I feel that they're likely to cost too much, are too busy, don't really care and just want to make me sit around and wait for them and then when it's my turn they just want to hurry up and get me out. The doctors I am most comfortable with are often in downtown or old town locations in small offices 30 years old or older, they are clean but not sterile-looking and people smile when you walk in and aren't too busy for a bit of small talk. This may not be the same for you, but you'll know a good practice when you see one. When I find an office that looks inviting – I take the invitation and walk in and just, well, start chatting up the receptionist. I mention that I am looking for a new practice and would she or he mind if I ask some questions. It can be anything, really (I've already called and done the background check, so this is just my chance to see how they are in person – but I stick to healthcare questions). I may ask how they treat patients without health insurance, what their payment policies are and what an average appointment costs without insurance, etc. I won't spend too much time, just enough to get a good feel for the place – are they friendly, are the staff actually knowledgeable? Again, you'll know it when you see it.

Of course the best bet at getting a good feel for a potential new doctor would be to speak to him or her in person, but this isn't always possible – they are, after all, very busy with some pretty important matters and their first priority is to the patients they already have. You'll have the most luck being able to at least meet the doctor, if not chat for a few short minutes, if you pop into their practice first thing in the morning or last thing in the evening when they are the least busy.

In today's world we all want to find people who are loyal to us and yet it seems that loyalty on our part counts for next to nothing. I tell you this because of what I am about to say. If you still have a handful of doctors you are considering, number them with your favorite as number one and so on. If you absolutely cannot make a choice between your remaining options when the time comes just go ahead and set up an appointment with your first choice. When it comes time for your next appointment if you didn't get a great feeling from doctor number one, make an appointment now with doctor number two. You aren't going to hurt anyone's feelings and your comfort, care and well being are more important than a bit of hurt feelings anyway.

We got lucky with our new family practitioner. We narrowed it down to two or three and hit the jackpot with number one! We really love her, she is way beyond competent, compassionate, and kind and has a very good staff of stodgy, but professional office members and sweet and capable nurses who get it right every time! And although we've never seen any of her partners, some of my friends have and I've heard good things about them, too.

We, however, did not get that lucky with finding a family dentist. That one that I'd mentioned a little while ago -Dr. Ms. Ego? It took a lot of hard work to find her -that's why I was so devastated when I saw her record and at first glance thought we'd have to leave her, too. We went through at least three dental practices in a year's time prior to finding our beloved One. We would see one dentist just one or two times before they would start haggling me about thousands of dollars worth of work they claimed my children needed. Things that were, in my opinion, completely unnecessary. Not to mention, way out of my budget.

I actually had one dentist refuse to prescribe antibiotics for my son's oral infection unless I agreed to let him do the procedure he wanted to do that day. I told him that I wanted to use the medication first to see if his condition improved and also to talk things over with my husband -I try never to make big ticket decisions on the spot. It's best for me to think it over away from the doctor's office or discuss it with my husband, or family or friends, just to be sure. I always prefer safe to sorry! At any rate, the receptionist felt so bad for me and also couldn't believe that the dentist refused a prescription for a patient who obviously had an infection and pain, so she told me to stay put and she would ask another dentist at the practice. It seemed she knew the one I'd had a row with was leaving for the day after my appointment, so she waited a few minutes and then asked someone else. Luckily the other doctor scribbled out a prescription without much ado and we were on our way -to the pharmacy and to finding yet another dental practice.

Although we got lucky in finding our primary care physician rather easily, it was still a little iffy as far as affordability, at first, so I still checked into state and county healthcare facilities. When I was growing up there was a real stigma attached to "the type of people" who go to free clinics. Isn't that the place where hookers and weirdoes go? While some people may still feel this way, free clinics have come a long way. Many of them have a wide range of services for local residents, good equipment (I wouldn't say state-of-the-art, but definitely up-to-date and in good working and reliable condition). Some areas may even offer more than one option for alternative healthcare. I checked all the usual places – Internet, phone book, and newspaper – to see what I could find under "healthcare". For state or county-run clinics or practices you may need to look in the "Government" section of the phone book.

I have a friend who just moved close by a couple of years ago. When she and her son relocated here she was on a tight budget – being a single mom and in a new area with a new job will do that! Her new insurance hadn't kicked in yet and she'd not had time to find a physician for herself or her eight-year old son, so when he got sick less than a month after their move she didn't know what to do. Luckily, she found out about the county free clinic here and called to find out when they could see her son. After their appointment she reported back that everything went great – the facility was clean and the staff was friendly and helpful. In fact she was so impressed she resolved to volunteer a few hours here and there to give back to her new community.

A neighboring county of mine used to have a practice called

AltMed where anyone could walk in and be treated for a variety of things. No appointment, insurance or referrals needed. It was really expensive though – but sometimes the convenience is worth it. Time is money – no matter what you do for a living or how busy your life is. You really have to weigh your options and do the math; a $50 appointment that has you missing three hours of pay from your work at $20/hour will really cost you $110, whereas a $75 appointment that keeps you from just one hour's work only costs you $95. On the other hand if money is really tight and you're currently unemployed, the $25 difference between the appointment costs may be worthwhile for you to spend the additional two hours at the doctor's office – just be sure to bring a good book!

Another alternative I frequently look into is pro bono or charity healthcare. Usually finding free medical services that aren't associated with the state or county facilities are a bit trickier and are typically reserved for specialty services. I don't easily find freebies for emergencies or short-term treatments for the common cold, flu and other ailments like that. What they are good for are things like annual physicals, cholesterol screenings, vaccinations, mammograms, cancer screenings, etc. It's a great way to have the bod checked out if you are worried about potential problems.

Last year my doctor found a lump in my breast. Gulp! She was nearly 100 percent certain that it was just some fatty tissue that was swollen due to my menstrual cycle, but she gave me a referral for a sonogram in the event that it worried me and I wanted to check it out for certain. (She also recommended I do my self-breast exams a bit more rigorously so that I could gage if it was cyclical or totally out-ofthe-blue.) At any rate, I have the referral still sitting here on my desk – mocking me in fact, it has become quite irritable from it's never-changing vantage point for the past 12 months. When I could no longer stand its taunts I decided to find out about getting an official mammogram. I'm not at the age where annual mammograms are recommended yet, but I think having one now just for peace of mind would be a good idea. So I logged on to the Internet and just typed in "free mammograms northern Virginia" and to my surprise several sites popped up. I located four or five valid, current sites that were offering this service in my area. Some of them are limited time offers as they are part of a traveling healthcare program.

I'm certain that if you search for free services in your area you'll find a surprising number of health services you can take advantage of, too, but be prepared to drive to the nearest metropolis. I didn't find many freebies that were right at my doorstep. I found a few that were within 20 miles, but most were in Washington, D.C., which isn't all that convenient, but it's really not too far when you consider the benefits.

I advise keeping all of these alternatives on record somewhere in your personal files. Your leftover suitable doctor picks; state and county facilities, alternative practices and pro bono services may not be needed right now, but they may all come in handy at some other time in the future. I like to take advantage of as many of these as possible – why pay your doctor $50 when you can pay the county nothing? Also, should something major arise – a need for surgery or a scary diagnosis – I have a list of resources I can turn to for a second opinion.

If I've learned one thing for sure, it's to always get a second opinion when it matters. I always know "when it matters" by my reaction to doctor's news. If the doctor gives me news of something surprising, shocking, scary or completely dreadful and I either cry or lose sleep or both – it matters. If the doctor tells me something I just don't think sounds right, or I'm skeptical at all (which is a lot of the time -but that's just me) – it matters.

I'm going back to my old premise that you won't hurt their feelings and even if you do – so what, your health and peace of mind is way more important. I can't stress enough how important a second opinion is. Last year when my son was diagnosed with a cyst/tumor in his gums that had to be surgically removed I was beside myself. I was really worried but not nearly as mortified as when we went to see the surgeon our dentist sent us to. She looked at the dentist's X-ray and then checked out my son's mouth for herself (very briefly and only with the naked eye -no equipment or instruments) and declared that yes, indeed, he had a cyst and it would have to be removed along with two teeth. She also informed us that first he would need to have a CT scan that we would have to bring back to her and we needed to move stat for the sake of my son's health! She said she would book an OR at the local hospital and perform the surgery under anesthesia. And that it needed to be done ASAP -it was *that* important. Then I asked a question innocently -not knowing I was rocking the boat, "How much will this cost?"

"I don't really know," she replied.

I asked her just to give me a ballpark figure and explained that we don't have health insurance and that we would be paying for everything out-of-pocket and needed to prepare for the expense. She persisted that she had absolutely no way of knowing what it would cost: there were her fees, the cost of the CT scan, the hospital fees, the anesthesiologist fees, etc. and she didn't know what the others would charge.

Then my husband spoke up, God bless him!

"You have done this before, right?!"

She nearly fell over. If I hadn't been so scared for my son I would have laughed -her expression was priceless -I have never loved my husband more. Of course she had, several times, she said.

"Then tell us what you *think* it will cost, approximately -you must know," he persisted.

She came up with a nice round figure of "oh, about $10,000 - 15,000." It was my turn to nearly fall over.

When my husband scraped me off the floor a second time (while muttering curses upon this woman who had made us wait two hours to give us this information) we left. I cried myself to sleep for a week I was so scared. I started looking into CT scans when it dawned on me – who was that woman? She was an upscale doctor in an upscale practice located in a large city who was used to dealing with the blessed moneyed masses that dwell close to our nation's capital. Luckily, specialist referral consultations like these are typically free of charge – they are really just checking out what your doctor has diagnosed and getting a good idea for the services that they will need to render.

The next night I told my husband I wanted to get a second opinion. He said, "Why? The next doctor is just going to tell you the same thing?" My reply was that I would really feel more comfortable if they did, then I would KNOW that we were having the right treatment for our son and if they didn't offer the same information then I would weigh the two against a third opinion until I felt comfortable with putting my child in their hands. He agreed. (Trust me, I'm getting to the point and you will definitely see the benefits of getting a second opinion when I get there!)

I started my new list of possible surgeons to interview. I picked a handful and researched their licenses but one of them really stuck out in my mind and I couldn't figure out why. He just seemed familiar, so when he checked out I made an appointment for my son to see him. It didn't take me long into the appointment to realize that he was the very surgeon who removed my wisdom teeth when I was a teenager – I immediately felt more at ease. He gave me the same diagnosis as the dentist and first surgeon had except that he seemed to think that although the surgery needed to be done soon, it was no big deal. This did reassure me, but also made my heart sink just thinking of the financial sacrifices we would have to make for this treatment. I asked him if our next step was the CT scan and he gave me a weird look and asked why I would bother with one of those. He admitted a CT scan would be nice to have but that it really served no purpose in this case. I began to brighten.

Then I asked if he would be performing the surgery at the hospital (it was right next door to his office – pretty convenient) and he gave me that weird look again. I told him where I'd been and what had been said to me and he began to understand where all of my misconceptions had come from. As it turns out he is not a big fan of the people I had been to (again, a point for the new guy!). He said that I was standing in a surgical center and that the hospital had no particular advantage to him since he had everything he needed in his own practice. This time I had to be scraped off the ceiling – a much better feeling, I assure you. I went for the gusto – how much would it cost us? I could see his fingers wiggling as he muttered some numbers and math equations in his head – about $1400 he said. I nearly giggled.

When we got home I told my husband about how not-scary this second doctor was, how he was so reassuring, personable, reasonable and comfortable. But the more at ease I felt the more a creeping sensation of "Is this too good to be true?" came over me. What if I just liked him more, what if he was telling me what I wanted to hear just so he could "win the job"? When I finally got over myself I realized that he really was a Godsend and that the first surgeon had just scared me so much that I wasn't thinking straight. We booked the surgery with opinion number two and I was a basket case. You have no idea what fear is until a child you brought into the world is taken to a room, sedated and prepped for surgery. I smiled until he went under and then I crumbled. I cried in the waiting room for a few minutes and then I blubbered out on the sidewalk outside the office building. When I nearly gained my composure I went back into the waiting room. For a grueling total of about 20 minutes did the surgery last. About 3 minutes after I came back inside the doctor informed me that my son was done, had woken up and was chatting the ear off one of his nurses! I have never been so happy in all my life – save the days he and his brother screamed their way into the world. (Also expensive medical days!)

I thank God every day that I stood my ground and got that second opinion. In fact I'm also thankful that we didn't have insurance during this ordeal. When I think about it I realize that if we'd had insurance we probably would have taken the first surgeon at her word and done everything she asked without question – we would have let the insurance company sort it out, pay for it and not really questioned it. For some reason having health insurance made us much more trusting (or maybe just oblivious) people. When you live without insurance you become much more scrutinizing – which really pays off especially in times like these. I am especially grateful that things turned out the way they did because I have little faith that my son's surgery would have gone as smoothly with the first doctor – just her bedside manner made me doubt her skills.

I know it was babbly, but that's my lesson on second opinions. Imagine if my son's condition had been more dreadful, or God-forbid, life-threatening and we hadn't looked into our options. By spending two weeks studying, researching, asking questions and getting a second opinion we spent only about 10 percent of the estimate the first surgeon gave us. Better yet, we found a better doctor who truly cared, who made us feel comfortable – and let me tell you medical procedures do not go well when a 9-year old is nervous to the point of screaming, crying and jumping out of his skin! We would have gladly spent the $10,000 if the first doctor had made us feel the way the second one did – the health and safety of our son was our primary concern and worth whatever we needed to pay. Luckily the good doctor came with good rates – that won't always happen but it's sure nice when it does.

Chapter 4: Get It In Writing

Rule number one of being a consumer and living in America: get it in writing. It really doesn't matter what the subject is; in a nation whose motto is "buyer beware" the buyer had better do whatever he or she can to protect him/herself.

If you think about it, we (consumers) probably ask lots of professionals to put their fees in writing and many of them do so without having to be asked. I've noticed in the past few years that whenever I take my car to a garage they generally have their rates posted in the waiting area. On top of that whenever you have work done they always provide you with a written estimate, prior to starting the job, of the cost of the parts and the approximate number of hours they expect the job to take.

When you have work done on your home, whether it's an appliance repair, leaky toilet or having your kitchen completely remodeled you expect the contractor to put their estimate in writing, right?

So why wouldn't you have the same expectations of your healthcare professionals? I do and I feel that they should expect to be asked to do this. I am always very wary of any practices that won't give their rates ahead of time. If they seem put out by this or flatly refuse then I won't use them for any reason. My assumption is that if they aren't forthcoming with their prices then they are used to charging enormously inflated rates and expecting their patients or their patients' HMOs to pay them without question. Another pitfall is that once you've had the procedure or treatment and get the bill, it's very difficult to negotiate. They will say that they've already done the work and you agreed to let them – you've received the benefit of their expertise, and so they will consider that if you agreed to treatment without a set price then you have also agreed to their rates even if you aren't aware of what they are.

At any appointment I make I ask what the cost will be, especially if it's a doctor I've never seen before or for a treatment I've never had done before. Most of the time the receptionist will have to look through a booklet, rate sheet or computer data in order to find out what each part of the visit will cost without the aid of health insurance. I try to always get this in writing because I typically find that on the day of the appointment the prices have changed – either because a different staff member is doing the pricing or because the quote didn't include everything or included too much – you never know.

I can't tell you the number of times my family has been quoted one thing and then charged another at the time of the doctor's visit -and 99 times out of 100 it isn't in our favor. After a few of these incidences I've become glaringly aware that getting a quote just isn't enough: it

MUST be in writing. I try not to let the doctor and his staff feel like I don't trust them. I always remind them that I have no insurance and that everything will be an out-of-pocket expense for me and so I can't have any surprises – I need to know exactly what to expect. They normally don't mind.

At this point I also stress how burdensome paying out of pocket can be and request that if there's anything they can do to reduce the price it would really be helping my family out. Most of them can't do anything without the doctor's approval, so sometimes I have to wait around a bit until the office staff can get together with the doctor to see if they are willing to give any discounts. At any rate, I do whatever I can to get the cost of the next visit nailed down before I leave otherwise I run the risk of facing a bill I find to be unreasonable on the day of the appointment. Should this happen, I know they'll hold me responsible for paying for the time-slot reserved even if I don't follow through with the treatment.

Here's the trickier part though: I don't just want them to give me the prices, I want them to write it down on something official like a prescription pad, business card, piece of letterhead or voided receipt – something that has the practice's name on it. If possible I try to get the staff member giving the quote to initial it. I just put on my best friendly face and let her know that it's just in case I have any trouble with the billing later, I will want to be able to prove that the price is correct, came from the practice and isn't just something I made up and wrote down myself. If the person giving the quote is hesitant to do this, I'll ask her if perhaps she can get a co-worker to verify her prices to make sure she has gotten everything correct before she commits to it, or maybe the doctor can review it and initial it for her. I find that doctors are a lot less wary to sign or initial things. They typically trust their staff members and don't have a lot of time for trivial matters like paperwork, so they're pretty quick to sign off and move on to waiting patients.

My younger son has had a series of dental appointments – he's just one of those kids that are plagued with cavities and other oral issues. At one point he needed to have a baby molar pulled, one that wouldn't have naturally fallen out until a few years later. For this reason the pulled tooth had to be accompanied by the installment of a spacer; a metal bracket attached to the adjacent tooth that has a metal arm reaching into the neighboring hole to ensure the other teeth don't scootch over and invade the space the adult tooth will need in a few years when it's ready to make it's untimely appearance.

At any rate, I asked our dentist's receptionist to please (and, yes, I say 'please' and 'thank you' every time!) write down all the costs associated with my son's next visit, when the pulling and spacing would be done. After a bit of searching she came up with a price in the $200 range – an estimate that she kindly wrote down for me on my receipt for that day's expenses. Although too much money in my opinion, I had gotten used to all of our dental appointments costing me through the nose (or teeth, as it would appear).

When the next appointment ended the receptionist handed me a bill for over $400. I panicked -our appointments there had always cost what we had been quoted before and so I didn't bother to bring my written estimate with me that day. (Hint: learn from my mistakes always bring your written estimate in with you to your appointment.) I tried to be patient and keep my cool. I explained that the estimate she had given me was merely half that price and that I was not prepared to pay that much money, again reminding her that without insurance it was all coming out of my personal budget and income and that I might have sought an alternative treatment (or dentist) had she given me that price to begin with. Being the near-saint that she is, she looked through my son's file for any evidence of her estimate. She said she remembered writing it down for me but not what the amount was.

I was about to suggest that I mail them the payment with a copy of her quote after I got home and found it, when she pulled a copy of it from my son's file. Apparently when she wrote it down for me it was on a carbon copy of my receipt and so was on the copy they kept in the office as well. The dentist was involved at this point and let the receptionist know what she had left out of the estimate but told her to honor whatever it was that she had quoted me. I know that she felt cheated and a bit upset at the $200 her staff member's error had cost her, but she is an honest and honorable, caring professional and she treated me the way she would want to be treated and I let them both know how much I appreciated it.

This could easily have been one of those frustrating situations that elevates to the point of anger, harsh words and never returning on my part, but then again, I chose this dentist because of her demeanor, expertise and professionalism, so it shouldn't have been a surprise that she treated me well. When you are careful in choosing your healthcare professionals and careful with how you do business with them, it really does pay off.

The last thing I try to consider when getting estimates in writing is what *else* this treatment means. I always ask the person giving me the quote if there is more to this procedure than meets the eye. For example, will there be bills coming to you from other parties like a medical laboratory or an anesthesiologist? Will there be follow-up appointments or treatments necessary? Will there be any prescriptions associated that I will need to have filled? I want to know about all of the *extras* that the estimate may not include.

When my older son saw that hoity-toity specialist and she dropped the $12,000 bomb on us, she also let us know that that price didn't include the CT scan she needed. Before we went for our second opinion I started calling around to find out what a CT scan would cost. As I recall I got estimates over the phone from a few hospitals and the price of the scan ranged from around $600 to $1600 -a tremendous range for the exact same service. But it wasn't until the third or fourth call that anyone mentioned to me that the price of the scan didn't include the radiologist's reading fee. I have never heard anything so ridiculous -they charge you one price to DO the scan and another *mandatory* fee to READ the scan and tell you what it means! I asked if there was a way to just have the scan and let the doctor performing the surgery read it -after all, it was really for her anyway, not for me. They assured me that no scan leaves their possession without their radiologist's reading. I had to call all of the hospitals again to check on this and they all said the same thing, so this time when I asked what the scan AND the reading would cost together the estimates ranged from approximately $1200 to over $2000. It just goes to show you how meticulous you have to be in your questioning. The surgery estimate did not include the price of the scan and the price of the scan did not include the cost of the professional reading. So take care to ask questions you may think are silly or trivial, because you never know what you're up against and it's difficult to anticipate what questions to ask when you are faced with a treatment you know nothing about. The best advice I can give in this scenario is to do more than ask questions, start a conversation with a person who has a lot of information to offer and just try to pick their brain. Be sure to ask them if there are things they know about that you haven't thought to ask or if there are other costs that aren't apparent to you.

Another great example of the need to get complete estimates in writing is another unfortunate experience my family has been through. To this day my husband still has not had the root canal he went to the dentist for about 10 years ago finished. The reason: he was quoted a figure for the entire root canal procedure; he went in for the root canal but they only did half of the treatment, asking him to return after a week to complete the process. When he went in to have the procedure completed they tried to charge him more money. He argued with them that the quote they gave him was supposedly all-inclusive for everything that was to happen from beginning to end, but they refused to take him at his word and honor theirs – so he left and never went back.

The problem was that the estimate he obtained was an oral one; had he gotten the quote in writing they would either have been able to point out that the estimate did not cover the follow-up appointment or he would have been able to point out to them that the quote was all-inclusive. Either way, they would have had an official estimate to fall back on. Without the price in writing it was really a lose-lose situation –

they lost a patient and my husband went without the care he needed due to the dishonesty of one doctor's staff.

Chapter 5: Money Talks: How to Find the Deals

Negotiating

If there's one thing my children have taught me it's that EVERYTHING is negotiable – allowance, punishments, bedtime, dinner – but your healthcare? Actually, that's negotiable just like everything else. We, as adults, are often prepared to negotiate prices at farmer's markets, garage sales, auctions and maybe even the antique store, but did you know that you can haggle with doctors, dentists and hospitals, too?

Healthcare providers are just like everybody else in this world, they are human beings doing a job to earn a living. They will charge what they feel the market will bear (and sometimes what the HMOs dictate) and their fees are not set in stone. Some larger practices have set fees that they will not stray from, but for the most part doctors have the power to adjust their prices if they feel the need.

I truly believe that everyone in the world should learn to negotiate -it's not panhandling, begging or being pathetic, it is about being realistic and reasonable and spending your money wisely. If you think about it, what you are saying by negotiating is that you have a desire for what someone else has (either a good or a service) but its worth to you is limited. The goal is to find the price that you are comfortable spending -you feel the good or service was *worth* what you paid -and a price that the person offering the good or service is willing to accept -they feel they were paid well for what they gave. If the price is too low the donor feels cheated and unhappy and if the price is too high the recipient feels duped and discontented. The key is to find that happy medium whereby both parties feel good about the exchange.

You would be surprised how much of your life will benefit by adopting this belief. I, myself, have gotten to the point where when I feel things -like groceries and clothing -are too expensive I simply do without unless I can find a way to negotiate a lower price. Naturally this doesn't work in retail stores -Old Navy will not agree with me that the great jeans I found there are really only worth $20 to me. I simply find new ways to get what I want for the price I'm willing to pay. Are the same jeans on eBay? Are there similar jeans at a discount store? Do I really *need* a new pair of jeans anyway? (I know my husband's answer to this already.)

It always amazes me when my family has their annual yard sale how many people will ask what the price of an item is and then just walk away. I stand there thinking to myself, "If you were really interested in that and you thought I was asking too much, why didn't you just ask if you could pay less?" It's a yard sale, for gosh sakes -I'd have said yes to 90 percent off just so I didn't have to take the item back into the house later. But so many people are just too embarrassed to negotiate; they simply pay what is asked of them or they go without the things they want. I have never understood that frame of mind, but I know people who feel that way, as if negotiating is beneath them. They feel that if they can afford it, they'll pay full price even if they don't think whatever the item is is worth the asking price. Or they just turn their backs and forget about the whole thing.

"Women, in general, are not very good at negotiating," offered Nancy Dailey, Ph.D., sociologist and award-winning author, "We're good at negotiating for others, but not for ourselves."

According to Dailey, girls are raised to be humble, modest and yet be the cheerleaders for those around them. Unfortunately that translates into adult females who have the innate ability to defend and fight for others more comfortably than they do for themselves. It is something that women, especially, need to overcome and Dailey recommends taking on the task of negotiating the costs of our healthcare as if we are taking care of it for someone else.

It makes a lot of sense. Although I've always been a tight-wad negotiator, I sometimes have trouble asking the right questions and trying to avoid conflict and confrontation instead of just being straightforward when it comes to getting information from doctors. My husband, who was upset one day that I had come home from a doctor's appointment without all of the pertinent information, reminded me that I have been a reporter for several years and that I routinely meet with strangers and ask them all kinds of probing questions without the first hint of worrying what they might think about me. The difference there, I explained, was that I am asking questions so that I can get the right information to write a great article that my editor and readers will be happy with and not because the information is essential to me personally.

Exactly the point, he said. I was handling it personally and so I was getting flustered, backing down and not getting out of it what I could. The next time I went to the doctors I came with a list in my hand of questions. I listened and took notes and didn't leave until I was satisfied. Negotiating prices for your healthcare should be handled the same. It's not personal, it's business. As clichéd as that sounds, it really is the way to go. While that $200 invoice is very personal to you and could be the difference between paying your heating bill or not, it's a matter of business to the doctor or treatment center. For the most part emotional reactions on your part will get you nowhere. The only way that a personal-emotional plea may get you the deal you want is to invoke a sympathetic emotional response from the person you're negotiating with.

The best way to go about it though, is to decide ahead of time what your optimal pricing solution would be and then what you would be willing to settle for. Hopefully the end result will be somewhere in between, but you have to go into it with a plan and a straight spine.

My advice: always go for what you want. You might not always get it, but you'll *never* get it if you don't try. My other pearl of wisdom: there's never any harm in asking.

Competition

In many cases, doctors operate under the premise that because your health is so important and because they know things you don't, they can charge you what they want and you'll pay it without question. So many people are afraid to "rock the boat" and doctors can take advantage of this at times. What you need to realize is that: yes, what a doctor can do is very valuable, indeed, but there is a limit to the value of their services, certainly a limit to your budget and there is no end to the amount of competition in the medical marketplace. Remember all of those hundreds of doctors you had to shuffle through to find this one? Well, they're all still out there and are able to perform the same services as your doctor.

Competition is the consumer's gift in the free marketplace use it.

The first step is applying what you learned in the last chapter: - get it in writing. Whenever I set up an appointment I find out what it's going to cost. Then I use that as a base price. Next I'll ask a staff member, or the doctor (even better) if they can bring the price down any. They might give me a discount just for asking, but sometimes I can use things like paying cash as an incentive -many businesses will give discounts for payments made within ten days or payments made the same day in cash; your doctor might, too.

Coupons

Another thing I've noticed is when a doctor changes locations or starts his or her own practice, expands their practice or is just looking for new business they will sometimes issue coupons. I find that a good place to find this is in the local newspapers, regional parenting/family magazines, mailer packets and the phonebook. Nearly every phone book has a coupon section and nearly all of them go unnoticed. They are typically things like discounts on engine work, air conditioning repair, pest control, etc., but sometimes there are also some for medical work. As I say this I am scanning my local phonebook to see what I come across. There's an offer for a $20 complete back examination, including X-rays. Discounts on an eye exam and glasses or contacts. Not bad for 30 seconds of research -next time I get a crick in my back, I know where to go!

Lab Work

My primary care physician gave me a tip for getting a deal on lab work. She said that there are now medical laboratories on the Internet that will allow you to order your own blood work without a doctor's orders and that they are sometimes less expensive than the labs a doctor uses and can save you the expense of a doctor's visit in order to get that lab order.

A while ago I suspected that I may have Lyme Disease, thanks to a deer tick that I pulled off my side and the extreme fatigue and vision changes I started to experience a few weeks later. So, I decided to try this new concept in lab work. I went online and found several web sites where you can order your own blood work. Naturally they had so many lab tests to offer that I didn't really know what I needed.

One phone call to my doctor later and I had the name of the test I needed. One of the lab sites I found charged $180 for the Lyme test I sought and another estimated about $220. This did not sound cheap to me, but I took notes so that I could compare.

The procedure was basically: fill out the online form and select the tests you wish to have, pay for the tests with your credit card online, print out the form and take it to your local affiliated laboratory and have them draw your blood.

The problem I ran into was that I couldn't locate a medical laboratory near me that would accept these lab forms. There were about five local labs and the first two I called said I could go ahead and order the lab work and pay for it online, but that I'd still need to have a doctor's orders before they would touch me. So, while I had the lab on the phone I asked them what they would charge me for a Lyme test if I were to get a doctor's orders and just pay them directly. The medical lab that was closest to my home (and my primary care doctor) quoted me $85.

When she asked about my insurance, I told her that I had none and she immediately gave me the phone number to her billing department and told me to ask them if they would give me a self-pay discount. I called the number and they told me that if I paid for the lab work the day I had my blood drawn they'd give me a 30% discount. To me, that's pretty significant.

It turned out that my doctor was willing to give me a lab order without having to come in for a visit, which I took advantage of, had my blood drawn and paid only $63 for the tests.

So, in this case, my doctor was wrong. It was much less expensive for me to deal directly with our local medical laboratory. It may not always be that way. If, for example, you live in a larger metropolitan area you may find that lab fees are more expensive and that many of them do accept on-line self-ordered labs. It's nice to have the option, even if it's not always the most economical. That's really an important lesson to learn -keep all of your options open and have alternatives in mind, you never know when you might need a good Plan B. Having more information can only help you in the long run.

Barter

It may seem medieval but my family has a lot of luck with using the barter system as well. Typically you'll have to speak to the office manager or the doctor in order to make this work, but we've discovered that chances are my family possesses some skill that our doctor might value. Perhaps they are presently understaffed and I could help out with the paperwork or answering phones for a few hours or maybe they need publicity in the form of a press release or an updated web site. I try to think of anything I could do that a doctor will value equally to that of their own services. The barter system works best if you've known your doctor a while -long enough that they are apt to trust that you'll hold up your end of the bargain and do a great job.

When my children's dentist found out that I'm a writer she let me in on her passionate plans; she was starting a gourmet gift basket business and she needed someone to put together a holiday brochure to pass out around town and draw in new customers. She paid me half my fee in cash and the other half she applied toward my son's dental bill. We both got what we wanted and were happy -it was a great arrangement.

Of course my fondest memory of bartering with a healthcare professional is one that directly benefited me.

By the time I'd reached the 3rd grade (now you know it's going to be a long story, right?!) I needed glasses. They were not cool. I was not cool. And I resented them forever. Well, at least for the six years I wore them. At age 14 I promptly got a job at the local mall and spent my very first paycheck on contact lenses. Which I wore, and wore, and overwore for the next 15 years until my eye doctor told me that I'd given myself corneal ulcers from not washing and changing my lenses often enough (and let that be a screaming warning to those of you reading this through soft-lensed peepers!). So, back into four-eyes mode I went with my father's song floating though my brain, "Boys don't make passes at girls who wear glasses!"

Never mind that I was married with two kids, forget the passes, I just wanted to never wear glasses again. I decided that the only way to get what I wanted was to suck it up and get laser eye surgery. In order to be brave enough to go through with it, I needed to know EVERYTHING about it. The more I learned, the more I realized that it would make a great newspaper or magazine article for other weak-willed glasses-wearers like me out there.

I went to my then newspaper editor and she loved the idea of a story about what it's like to have laser surgery from the patient's perspective. I then went to the doctor who would perform the surgery as well as his affiliate who does all of the preliminary testing and eye-mapping and they both loved the idea of getting some free publicity. In return I got a discount of about 35 percent off the price of the surgery, which, if you've priced laser eye surgery, is a large chunk of change. By bartering for my surgery, not only was I able to bring the price of the procedure down to a more affordable amount, but it also boosted my confidence, which was necessary since I was really scared. I mean, what doctor is going to muff up a surgery that is being photographed and publicized?

It turned out to be a great trade all the way around (unless you count the fact that the newspaper lady stiffed me) -no more glasses for me, surgery that I could afford and free publicity for two local healthcare practices.

While not everyone can offer free publicity like I can in a barter situation, I believe that everyone possesses some skill that others can find value in. The key is to know what others want or need and be able to present the option of barter in an attractive way. For me, I realized that laser eye surgery is basically a 10-minute procedure and they do dozens of them every day. Armed with this knowledge, I was able to convince them that while the surgery meant a lot to me, income from one procedure on their part would not mean as much as the potential income from several other people who could find the confidence from my shared experience in the newspaper. In short, I tried to get the doctors to realize that they needed publicity to draw in more patients and that my article had the potential to bring them more business, which was enough to supplement the cost of my procedure.

I've always found that if I can present a barter situation to the person who has what I want in a way that makes them feel that they are getting an equal or better value by utilizing what I have to offer, then they are more likely to accept. It's also very important to know who to ask. Speaking to the office manager, receptionist or nurse is likely to get you nowhere. Approaching the doctor or senior practitioner is your best bet -they have much more decision-making power. I also never let anyone else barter for me. In other words, I would never ask someone who won't be making the decision to barter to present my case to their superior. Chances are they won't present my case as well as I will because it's not as important to them and they don't know what I have to offer as well as I do.

When trying to negotiate with your regular healthcare provider (someone that you will see once a year or more on a somewhat regular basis) don't be ashamed to let them know about your current situation; -remember they really are human beings, too. Tell them what an impact paying directly for health costs does to your budget. Most likely they will already have made an assumption about this since you don't have insurance.

Just Ask

In fact, it still amazes me the assumptions that medical practitioners and their staff will make about patients who don't carry insurance. My doctor caught me off guard at my last well-woman check up. When we came to the end of the exam -the question and answer section -I inquired about changing my birth control. I had stopped taking The Pill but didn't know which option to switch to -they are all objectionable in my mind, only marginally less objectionable than having another baby. To my surprise the woman who has required me to strip down to nothing but my wedding band for the past five years asked me how important birth control was: was I seeing anybody right now? Her assumption was that I must be a single mother to be suffering so financially and therefore sans health insurance.

The fact of the matter is that I had never said we were financially badly off and I certainly never told her I was a single parent. The fact that I was negotiating my own healthcare just insinuated that to her. I'm okay with people thinking I'm poor, but a whole lotta trouble comes about from people thinking I'm single!

Anyway, I always inform my healthcare providers of my insurance status and the fact that lower costs will be of great benefit to me, but I never give out more information than necessary. I won't throw myself a pity party or over-dramatize the situation, but I let them know that whatever they can knock off the bill is a great help to me and my family. And if you *are* a single parent, mentioning it may garner yourself a little sympathy discount.

Even if they can't deduct anything from the bill, they may be able to make alternative suggestions for keeping costs down in the future, like coming into their practice for my child's annual physical, but going to a clinic for free vaccinations, or maybe some of the laboratory work needed can be done at a less expensive lab -you never know, but they might.

Most doctor's offices require payment in full on the day of service for self-pay patients. Perhaps the cost of the services you receive really isn't out of line and they won't give you a discount, but they may be willing to take a deposit and work out a monthly payment plan. It's always easier to pay large bills in smaller chunks than to take the hit all at once, leaving you to worry and wonder where the money for rent, gas, groceries or electricity will come from this month.

Sometimes we skip the doctor's office altogether and find a better deal elsewhere. As I stated before, in Chapter 3, most large cities or counties have a free clinic where they can treat residents for little or no money. Just check with them first -if yours is like mine, they keep some wacky hours and they only do certain things on certain days. Also in my area now, one of the local retail chain drug stores is offering sessions with a nurse practitioner. It costs something like $10 or $15 for a walk-in appointment and they can dispense real medical advice, perform some tests and even prescribe medications. This would be the first route I would take if my child had some weird rash or I thought he was coming down with something common like the chicken pox or strep throat.

The great thing that getting the hang of negotiating does for me is to give me a sense of power and freedom. When I negotiate I never go into it blindly. I always have some sort of price in mind that I'd be willing to pay. If the person I'm negotiating with is asking more than I'm willing to pay then I have to decide whether or not I can live with paying more. In some cases I'll just tell them their price is unreasonable to me and I'll walk away. That is the most powerful thing you can do in a negotiation -walk away. You are holding firm to your ideals about your money and how you'll spend it and showing yourself respect. It really does feel very powerful.

Negotiating is a balance though, and you have to stay flexible. When I'm negotiating with a healthcare provider, chances are we aren't going to do a lot of back-and-forth, but if I tell them what I'd be willing or able to spend and they can come reasonably close to that figure then more often than not I'll acquiesce. But if they can't even come close I know I always have alternative options.

In most cases, I prefer sticking with doctors my family is familiar with, but if they don't have rates that we can afford I will first do some calling around to other practices to find out what other doctors charge for their services. If my doctor is more expensive than most others I will let them know what others are charging and that I can't afford their rates and see if they're willing to match their competitors. If not, then I have to decide how important it is and if I'd rather pay inflated rates or start searching for another doctor.

You won't always get what you want through negotiation, but it really can help and it's always worth a shot.

Chapter 6: Getting Your Meds

Long gone are the days of the neighborhood pharmacy, where you could walk up to your neighbor, who just happens to be the pharmacist and who also just happens to know everything about you, your family, your friends, your enemies and remembers every illness, ailment, rash and embarrassing situation each of you has ever had. Although having such vast knowledge, not to mention blackmail leverage, all contained in one being could be a bit daunting, it was also nice to know that you'd be well taken care of by someone who genuinely cared about your welfare. That personal relationship was one you could rely on and when it came time to filling prescriptions you could rest assured that your pharmacist would make sure you got exactly what you needed. In fact, he was probably as knowledgeable about which medications you needed as your physician and could make recommendations.

Unfortunately, today things are far more impersonal and I find I have many pharmacists, depending on which shops I plan on frequenting on the day I fill my prescription, or who has a deal going. And I promise you that any one of them has no idea who I am. If I've been there before, they'll likely have data saved in their computer, and they'll know my name, which medications I've had filled at their location in the past, and the fact that I have no insurance, but that's about the extent of their knowledge.

The point I am trying to make is that our pharmacists are really no longer familiar with us and our needs, nor are they truly looking out for our well being. (I will make an exception here, though, for the small locally owned and operated pharmacies. They are rare, but they do exist.) For the most part, however, pharmacists are strictly department or drug store employees who happen to have a degree and a license -otherwise they are the same as the other store clerks, trained to do as much business as possible in the least amount of time. As with all other aspects of shopping these days it's up to you to look out for yourself and your family.

The good news is that we, as consumers in the free world, have choices like never before. We have numerous places from which to purchase our medications: grocery stores, drug stores, department stores, pharmacies. We even have choices when it comes to which medications to purchase; there are now several brands of nearly every type of drug known to man, including generic versions and even several different types of medications for every ailment under the sun.

I am a strong advocate of self-education. I firmly believe that when a doctor prescribes a medication you should immediately (before calling it in) do some research on that particular drug to find out exactly what it was designed to do, will it fix the problem or just temporarily alleviate it, what are the side effects, what are its alternatives, and so on. Preferably, do some research on what it is you are experiencing that is causing your doctor to prescribe you these medications. In some instances a bit of Internet or library research can provide you with some great (not to mention cheap) alternative solutions to your problem. I can't tell you the number of times I have "fixed" myself and my children with remedies I've found on the Internet and in books, thereby saving myself the fees of a doctor's appointment AND the cost of medications.

A few years ago, during the fall soccer season, I noticed that my son was having trouble keeping up with the other kids on his soccer team; they were literally running circles around him. While I was aware that he's not necessarily the "athletic-type" I knew he wasn't naturally *that* slow. I also noticed that he was breaking down into coughing fits, sometimes while running around, but mostly at night in bed. It was even starting to happen at school. I began to suspect that he was developing asthma, but I didn't really want him to be diagnosed with the ailment, since that would mean a life-time of inhalers and possibly other medications, diminished physical activities (which I was already fighting since he's the book/computer/video game-type of child) and a stigma attached to him by classmates.

Determined to find another way, I plunked myself down at my computer and started digging through the Net to try to figure out what to do. As it turned out he had a very acute bout of asthma that was brought on by the use of central heating systems. The dust and air impurities that were being blown out through HVAC systems was impairing his ability to breath, causing his coughing fits at school and at home at night. Additionally, the heaters and drop in humidity were drying out the air and making it even worse. We immediately started humidifying the air at home and I downloaded a set of breathing exercises intended to make his lungs work more efficiently. It worked like a charm. By the spring season he was keeping up with his teammates on the soccer field and the coughing fits were gone. The kid just needed some moisture in his life. Being the skeptic that I am, I am certain that had I taken him to the doctor he would have diagnosed my son with asthma -he was exhibiting all of the signs and why not diagnose? After all a diagnosis like that comes along with a lifetime of increased doctor's visits and drug prescriptions.

Another example of saving money by doing your homework is last year when I started experiencing a tingling in my toes. It was the oddest sensation -it wasn't like my foot was going to sleep, it was more like the pins and needles feeling you get after your limbs start to wake up. I noticed it most when I was wearing my house slippers and I thought maybe the wooly fabric on the inside was just rubbing the bottoms of my feet the wrong way -so I stopped wearing them. My feet felt the best when I wore socks and my trusty old sneakers, which was not the fashion statement I normally go for, but it was comfortable.

After a week or two, though, the sensation in my toes started to worsen and began to occur in both of my feet. I got really worried and thought of seeing my doctor. My husband, in his normal nonchalant manner, told me I worry too much and that it was probably nothing. Easy for him, I thought, his toes haven't been tingly for two straight weeks.

My initial worry was that I was experiencing the onset of diabetes. Again, the thought of having a doctor officially diagnose such a troublesome disease frightened me more than my tingly toes, so I began to do my homework -on the Internet, of course. I found a slew of ailments that were could-be's but one that seemed to make a lot of sense to me -a pinched nerve in my lower back. I would never have thought that a sensation in my feet was an indication of a problem in my back and that it would have possibly been more beneficial to see a chiropractor than a physician.

After giving it further thought, it made a lot of sense: I had recently started Jazzercising at a new center with hard tile flooring (the previous center had nice floors that would give a little while constantly bouncing around for an hour a day). There were other indicators, too, that a pinched nerve made sense -things that I would never have thought to tell my doctor about because they just hadn't occurred to me before doing research.

At any rate, my research led me to a half a dozen stretching exercises meant to alleviate the pinched nerve in hopes of restoring it to it's regular position and I put myself on a strict regimen of stretching twice a day -more if I was feeling really stiff or tingly. And I kept wearing those unsightly sneakers day in and day out, they really did help my back with their snug fit, padded soles and good arch support.

It took a month or two for the nerve to free itself and my tingles to go away, but I was so relieved when it did.

Outcome: Investigating health issues on the Internet = zero dollars, self-diagnosis = zero dollars, downloading stretching exercises = zero dollars, stretching daily and wearing ugly shoes for two months = zero dollars. Restoring oneself to feeling like a million bucks = priceless!

One thing that really struck home with me was that I had found several problems that I could have been suffering from based on my symptom of tingly toes. I kept digging, though, until I found one that really seemed to suit me and my situation. How many times have you been to the doctor with one specific symptom and the doctor replied, "Well, that could mean many things, give me a few days and let me do some research on the topic, and formulate a questionnaire for you so that I can pinpoint the exact problem and treatment." ?

Typically, it never happens that way. Instead the doctor may indicate that your problem could be one of many things but they will narrow down the choices by treating the most common or probable ailment first and then if that doesn't work you'll return, still ailing and they'll move on to option number two. This is why I advocate for self-education. Even if you are convinced that you should see your doctor, do the research anyway. If nothing else it may bring up other symptoms that you are having that you wouldn't necessarily think are related or things that you've done that may be contributing factors of your problem. You may even find that you can determine what the problem is all by yourself. All of these things are helpful when face-to-face with your doctor; bring them all up. Even if you're wrong, you've given your doctor more information to go on, which will aid them in pinpointing your problem and an appropriate course of treatment.

Take my problem, for example. If I had just gone straight to the doctor before doing my homework all I would have been able to tell her was that I had tingly toes -that sensation you feel when your limbs are waking up. That's not much to go on and she may have assumed, based on what she knows about me, that I was pre-diabetic.

Take a different approach and when I felt all tingly and did my Internet delving and then went to the doctor I would have been able to tell her that I suspected I had a pinched nerve because my toes were a bit tingly, I Jazzercised three times a week on a very hard, unforgiving floor and I didn't seem to be as flexible as I had been just a few months prior. This certainly gives a totally different perspective on the situation.

It's exhilarating when you are able to make a proper self-diagnosis and solve your own woes without spending a dime, but had I continued to feel badly even after a couple of months of my stretching I would have eventually gone to see the doctor assuming that I either wasn't alleviating my poor nerve or that I had misdiagnosed my problem in the first place. Had I done so, I imagine some sort of prescription would have ensued.

Which would have sent me -yep, you guessed it -back on the Internet to find out what in the world I'd be taking. Since I am very drug-naïve, I look up any prescriptions I'm unfamiliar with (which is pretty much all of them). I am looking to see what the drug was made to do, what it's made out of and what complications are associated with it -side effects, killer combos when taken with other meds, etc. The next thing I want to do, assuming I didn't find any deal-breakers is to determine what the proper dosages are and make sure the doctor's prescription is in line with that. Then I look for the suggested retail price of the medication and what alternatives are currently on the market and their prices.

If I find anything objectionable -the dosage, the side effects, the cost, etc. I'll call the doctor's office and let them know that I'd like the doctor to change my prescription to a different dosage, or an alternative drug and let them know why. The doctor may come back with an explanation of why she chose that particular medication and how it's better than the alternative dosage or drug I've suggested or she may

58

uphold my concerns and give me a new prescription.

Whatever the outcome is, my next step is to begin calling around to find out who has the best deal in town. It may take a couple of days to find out -pharmacies can be very busy places and they may need to call back. My first question is always (and sometimes I can find out on-line more quickly): is this medication on the $4 prescription list? The $4 prescription list is a long list of drugs that many stores now sell for $4 for approximately a month's worth of dosages and $10 for a 90day supply in most cases. Many common drugs are on this list to make it more affordable for the masses (us) who have no insurance or insurance that doesn't cover drugs. This deal is available at Wal-Mart and Target pharmacies and a few other stores that want to compete.

The list is way too long to include here, but it includes many medications that are commonly prescribed like Amoxicillin, Naproxen, Albuterol, Nystatin, Prednisone and a whole bunch of others that I can't pronounce. Just type in the keywords: $4 Prescription List and you'll find some Wal-Mart and Target links to the list, which seems to be updated to add new medications several times a year. When I just looked at the list there were a full four pages of drugs on it.

If I can't get my prescription filled for $4, then I just keep calling to find out what other pharmacies are charging for the prescription. I also ask if any of them are running any specials or have coupons out for their store. At one point I kept seeing a Target coupon in the Sunday paper that announced if I brought them a new prescription they would give me a $10 gift card. It probably doesn't apply to the $4 drugs, but ten dollars off of my next purchase is a pretty good incentive (unless, of course, the prescription costs ten dollars or more above what others are charging).

Many stores have coupons on-line, too, so I'll do a quick search there as well as in the local papers and mailers.

Another alternative for medications is to find an on-line pharmacy. While this seems questionable to me, there are many pharmaceutical companies who can fill a prescription over the computer and mail medications straight to your door. This will work if you don't need the medications immediately and if the prices are low enough after the cost of shipping and handling is factored in to compete with your local pharmacies.

A quick search for the sake of this chapter and I found dozens of web sites claiming to be able to fill a prescription on-line, a few who claim to be able to do so without even having a prescription and others who are out of the country but willing to ship internationally. Although I no longer take birth control pills, that was the first common medication that came to my mind. I was able to find Tri-Cyclen 28-Day in a 3-pack (which would cover roughly three months of birth control) for $55. When I was taking birth control pills, I was spending about $25 per pack, which is a 28-day supply, so this appears to be a pretty good deal - like buying two and getting one free. The shipping fees at this particular site is $10 per shipment -so in this instance I would come out about $15 ahead every three months or $5 a month. While it seems small, I can take my family out for dinner or to see a movie for my $60 saved at the end of the year. You could save even more by ordering more at the same time. For instance if I bought four 3-packs, which would cover me for nearly a year the cost would be $220 for the pills and $10 for shipping or $230 total for a one-year supply of birth control. Whereas if I continued to purchase the pills one pack at a time at $25 each I would pay $300 each year. Plus if you want to get picky, by ordering on-line I am also saving myself the time it takes to drive to the store, hand in the prescription, wait around for it (or drive off and then back again), pay for it and drive back home - not to mention the cost of the gas to get me there and back twelve times.

I must admit, I've never ordered my medications through the Internet (surprising, since I do EVERYTHING else on the Internet!) but I think I've just convinced myself that this is the way to go. Unless, like I mentioned earlier, you need to start taking your medication immediately after the doctor prescribes it.

Just be careful and make sure you get the proper medications, in the proper dosages and if you can save yourself a few headaches, time and money in the process you may start to feel better even before popping the first pill!

Chapter 7: Seeking Alternative Treatments

If you take your kid to the doctor with a broken arm and he or she suggests setting the bone and putting a cast on, there's not much to discuss. If, however, your doctor says your child has a cyst hidden under his gums and will need to have oral surgery to remove the teeth and the cyst under general anesthesia -well, now we have something to talk about, think about and research (and you thought homework was a thing you left behind in high school!)

Many medical issues are not cut and dried. In the broken arm scenario, you are pretty certain you know what the problem is and what to expect as far as treatment goes, but very few diagnoses are so simple. For many medical situations you may know the diagnosis going in but not the treatments and for many others you may be unaware of what the diagnosis may be, yet alone what types of treatments go along with it.

If we are not under time restraints that require immediate and emergency treatment, I always try to get at least one other opinion. If for no other reason, I do it for peace of mind. If I find two doctors that make the same diagnosis and recommend the same treatment, then I know I am getting accurate information. If there is any discrepancy then I know further research is needed.

I believe that second opinions are a good idea especially when the first opinion comes from a specialist who's been referred by our doctor. Again, with the skepticism, I know, but I just get this nagging feeling that referrals are simply a way for our doctors to put money in the pockets of their friends. I consider referred specialists to be professionals we don't know well enough to truly trust and it's amazing how different each doctor is. They differ in diagnoses at times, in proposed treatments, in pricing, in personalities and on every other level. You know how you tried on many different dresses or tuxedos before choosing the perfect one for your wedding? Well, trying on different doctors is even more important.

"You should certainly take the recommendation from your primary care physician," said the Administrative Director of a healthcare facility in northern Virginia, "but also seek other options -often times doctors recommend old friends or colleagues. You can search the Internet for alternatives or ask your doctor for secondary referrals."

The Administrative Director also noted that if you don't have a primary care physician, then the Internet can be your new best friend.

"Look at where they went to school, how long they've practiced, how much experience they have with your condition and what general outcome patients with your condition who've seen this doctor have had, " he said.

For every opinion I get I ask the doctor if he or she can recommend alternative procedures. Something like, "Is this the only way to fix the problem or is this just the most common procedure or the one you are more familiar with?" Occasionally I find that there are alternatives -some may be more risky, less successful, or may be out of the realm of expertise of the specialist we are seeing.

"Always seek out a second opinion," advised the Admin. Director, "sometimes a third -they all have different philosophies on everything from treatments to surgeries."

I know I've harped on this example several times already, but it bears bringing up again -I learned so much from it. When my son's dentist told me that he had a cyst in his bottom gums that was causing two adult teeth to grow sideways down under the surface, thus preventing them from pushing up into their proper place, I was clueless. Even when she showed me on the X-ray, I really didn't know what to say, think or do. I could definitely see the teeth under the gums laying down instead of standing upright, but that black blob she showed me and called a cyst -it looked just like all of the other darkness visible on an X-ray.

She referred me to a maxillofacial oral surgeon -a great one, she assured me, one she went to college with and had known all of her adult life. It instilled instant trust in me. After all, we love our dentist why wouldn't we love her friend, too? What it should have instilled in me was a sense of skepticism.

The specialist's office was about an hour away, so we weren't all that happy when we arrived anyway, after having driven forever in outer D.C. rush-hour traffic. Then we waited......and waited.......and waited. While we waited, my husband paced back and forth, back and forth -oh, and back and forth in front of the receptionist's desk, making comments about how unprofessional it is to demand people come at a certain time and not be late and then leave them waiting. I believe after the first hour and a half he commented on what his bill would amount to for the time he wasted in the waiting room. We truly are every doctor's dream!

When she finally saw us it was after all of the other patients had gone home and her staff was brusque, to say the least, awaiting our departure so that they, too, could go home. Still, we were hopeful -and very worried about our son.

This referred surgeon was very curt with us and left us feeling angry, scared, worried and just plain low.

We left with all of the necessary paperwork and information and said we'd let her know when we had the CT scan. I think she was so happy to get us out of her office, she didn't charge us for the consultation. I went home and cried all night -she had really scared me. I was worried that the cyst would burst in the middle of the night or that my son would suffer some sort of permanent damage from waiting for treatment or botched surgery or never wake up from the anesthesia I was a mess.

A wise little voice popped up inside my head. I'm not sure how I heard it through the sobbing, but it told me to find another doctor, that waiting a few more days would be okay. I told my husband, the strong man with the wet shoulder, that I wanted to get a second well third, actually if you count the dentist as the first, opinion.

Naturally, I didn't know many maxillofacial oral surgeons, so I relied on my old friend -my computer, which was how I came up with the second surgeon, which we immediately set up a consultation with.

I went into the second consultation with the attitude that I already had one diagnosis and treatment plan and I was looking for anomalies in the story. I wanted to see if this doctor would say anything new or different that would make me discount the information I'd been given before. If not, I wanted to find out if there were any alternatives to the surgery that had been recommended.

He looked at the X-ray and my son's mouth and said, yes, he needs to have two baby teeth pulled, the cyst removed and under anesthesia. Ok - everything is the same. I feel better, relieved, assured.

Then he took another look at the X-ray and noticed the dentist's name on it.

"Oh, you're a patient of *her's*," he said with a bit of a sneer.

Uh-oh.

"Uh....yes....why," I stammered.

He wouldn't get into it but said that they just don't see eye to eye on some things. I immediately trusted him. After my experience with my dentist's crony, I welcomed the opinion of someone who owed her nothing.

He was such a great guy, he made my son feel comfortable, he made me feel comfortable (he even sat and told us stories about how his wife used to be just like me - running around trying to take care of two young, sometimes mischievous, boys). He did what I had, up until that point, thought impossible - he got me to stop worrying for a few moments. Although I knew otherwise, he treated us like we were the only patients in that day (and not like we were keeping him from doing something better).

It was amazing how different the two surgeons were - one was in a pretty, new building in the hub of city life, an upscale practice to be sure, with an uptight staff and a doctor who had no qualms about spending people's money like it made no difference. The other was an older, more laid-back doctor in an old brick building in a small town with a friendly staff and reasonable billing practices. What one estimated would cost us nearly $15,000 (which is money I assure you we didn't have on hand) we got from the other doctor for less than 10 percent of that amount and I am certain he did a better job than the first surgeon would have. Caring plays a big role.

The reason I included this long-winded recounting of my experience regarding my son's oral surgery was to show how important it is to ask questions, seek alternatives and persist at finding a comfort level. Although that first specialist is probably very skilled in her profession and she would have done a good job, we just weren't comfortable with anything about her: the distance she was from our home, the upscale practice she maintained, the attitudes of her staff, her own demeanor and her pricing.

I'm sure she's a perfectly good surgeon, but had we taken her at her word and scheduled the procedure, no questions asked, we would have gone through a lot more hassle (the CT scan and the hospital visit), had a negative experience resulting in even further skepticism on the part of my husband and myself and fear of doctors and treatment on the part of my son (she seemed to like inducing fear with her claims of immediacy) and we would have incurred a tremendous debt that would have hurt us financially for years.

While neither surgeon could come up with any alternative treatments to solve the problem of my son's cyst, the second doctor's treatment plan was much simpler, less costly and yet just as effective.

In this instance my research didn't bring much information about what to expect as far as treatments, but I did spend a good amount of time looking at the qualifications of the local surgeons.

Take my examples in the last chapter, however, about my son's case of asthma and my pinched nerve. In both of those cases, my Internet research led me to find alternative treatments that I could handle on my own. While this certainly isn't always the case, I use my research to help me understand what our doctor tells me and to help me determine what questions I should be asking.

My advice: ask as many questions as possible, even if they're silly ones. Remember how I asked the second surgeon about getting a CT scan and booking an OR? To him, those were ridiculous questions - he thought I was out in left field. Of course I was in left field, that first surgeon had left me there! But he was patient and kind and gave me answers to all of my questions - silly or otherwise. But when we had asked that first surgeon what seemed like a very simple and valid question (What will this cost?) she refused to even give an estimate, at first. That's a bad sign. If a doctor can't or won't give an estimate for any treatment then either they are out of touch with the accounting and billing side of their own practice or they are just so used to dealing with people who either let their HMO pay costs without question or for which money is no object.

"Too many times we give our power to the doctor and allow them to do what they want without questioning," said Dailey.

Dailey admitted that this is especially one of the pitfalls of having health insurance. It instills a sense of complacency and compliance. We trust too easily sometimes when we should be doing more questioning. As an example, Dailey remembered an incidence she'd run into when having her annual mammogram.

"What tends to happen is that if you have health insurance you're much more likely to get care you don't need," she said, "I go for routine mammograms every year and one time the doctor saw a spot she thought should be checked out and biopsied. The surgeon said that it was most likely nothing but because I had insurance I went ahead with the procedure and had the biopsy."

Dailey admitted that if she hadn't had health insurance she probably would have passed on the surgery after hearing the surgeon say it wasn't something he would have worried about. The procedure cost $7000, something that would have given her pause, but since her co-pay was only $400 she went ahead with it.

She also admits that it's difficult to make healthcare decisions based on dollar figures but "the problem is that there is so little information out there that is available for people to make educated healthcare choices."

I tend to agree to a certain degree. Certainly I feel out of my element at times when making healthcare choices for my family - no amount of research on my part will give me a medical degree, but I do know that there is a massive amount of pertinent and helpful information that can be found if you're willing to take the time. I find that the more research I do, the better armed with appropriate questions I am. And two heads are always better than one: I also find that if I bring my husband along, he may well annoy me but he can come up with a whole host of questions I never even thought of. Sometimes I'll even ask questions to which I know the answer. It gives me a better feel for the qualities and the qualifications of the doctor and ensures that I am not taking any information for granted.

I am aware of how many times the words "research" and "Internet" have come up in this book and I have to tell you that getting on-line really is the best way to find the most information quickly. If you do not have a computer or the Internet at your home, it would benefit you to go to your local library and spend a few hours searching the Net.

Sometimes Internet searches can be frustrating, leaving you feeling that you've been spinning in circles for a very long time and getting nowhere fast. Here are a few tips that I've found very helpful:

a.) in the search bar where there is a web address (http://something.html or www.something.com), delete that address and type a specific question. Ex. "Where can I get a free mammogram in Washington, D.C.?"

b.) if the search doesn't bring up anything you are interested in, try asking the question differently. Ex. "Washington, D.C. mammograms for free" or "free cancer screenings Washington, D.C."

c.) once a long list of sites with possible helpful information pops up, I start at the top and check out each site that seems reasonably helpful. If it's not what I want, I just hit the back button (sometimes a backward pointing arrow) and go back to the list.

d.) if my search takes me to any sites of agencies, organizations or companies that look like they have a lot of good information, I write down their name and contact information or print a page of their web site with that info on it, call them or email them and see if they have any other helpful health information. Ex. You've found a charitable health organization that performs free mammograms: call and ask them what other free services they offer, you may find that you can get your annual well-woman check-ups or other screenings there at the same time.

e.) if I start to get dizzy from going in circles, which I tend to do, frequently, and I get frustrated (visions of computer components flying through the air!) - I stop. Take a break. Sometimes it helps to start with the telephone, call the local free or county clinic or the state's health department and tell them what I'm looking for. They can often give me the name, phone number and/or web address of an organization who may be able to help me.

f.) I try to stay away from the commercial medical web sites that are specifically designed to help you diagnose medical conditions. In my experience I've found that they are too vague and tend to make me a basket case. Several times I went to a very popular medical site to see what was "wrong" with me and every single time I came out with a wrap sheet as long as my arm of things I "might" have and they were all scary, horrible, sometimes fatal things - every single symptom I typed in would ultimately lead me to cancer. I find it more helpful to find discussion forums where real doctors and real patients chat about a certain issue and you can see what lots of other people think and what they've experienced in similar situations. No one there is making any money based on their comments or referrals, they're just trying to help people by sharing their experiences.

If you absolutely cannot find a way to spend some time on the Internet to do your homework grab the telephone. Start with your doctor's office, the county clinic, the state health department, anyone you can find a phone number for who may have information. Call and describe what you are looking for and ask if they can give you any information or point you in the direction of someone who can. Talk to your friends and family and see if they, or anyone they know of, have been through something similar and ask lots of questions. Perhaps Aunt Mae's neighbor Sarah was just diagnosed with diabetes and you are afraid your tingly toes could be just that. Get her number and ask her how she felt before she was diagnosed. What were her symptoms? Did the doctor give her any pamphlets on the disease and how to recognize it? Realize that every human being is different and will have a different experience with any given issue, but it's a place to start and gather comfort and information. You'd be surprised how willing people are to share their experiences with others, it makes everyone feel better to share, so don't be afraid to ask.

Chapter 8: The Hospital

For most uninsured people, seeking treatment at a hospital is about the scariest thing possible. Many people believe that without insurance a hospital will do one of two things: give substandard care or refuse treatment altogether. In many cases uninsured individuals opt to go without the medical attention they need for fear of being turned away and humiliated or being treated but with contempt and in a shoddy manner.

This is really a hyped-up myth. Hospitals are not evil entities, they are businesses run by professionals who want to make money. Remember, though, that these professionals are all human beings, many of whom have taken oaths or chosen their profession to help people who are in need of medical attention. Hospitals (all that I know of anyway) will not turn uninsured patients away or treat them any differently than patients who have insurance. If you find a doctor or hospital that gives less care to an uninsured patient than he or she does to an insured patient, you will have it made in the shade for life -can you say Malpractice Lawsuit?

What I like to do, however, is scope out all of the nearby hospitals. Maybe *like* isn't the right word, but I feel the *need* to know as much about the facilities near me as possible so that when (and hopefully never) my family needs medical care through a hospital, I'll know which one to make a bee-line for.

Although they will mostly treat their patients the same regardless of insurance, they are all different from each other. It's like choosing which wireless company to use for your cell phone service you have a few to choose from and they basically do the same thing but some of them have nicer care centers, better staff, better customer service or better pricing.

"It is exactly the same for us to treat a patient with or without insurance here," said the Administrative Director of the treatment facility he runs, "We have a charitable outlook and take care of anyone who comes to the center seeking help."

He also noted, however, that smaller practices may turn uninsured people away, but that most hospitals and larger facilities won't. Additionally, he mentioned something that's very important for patients and care facilities to remember: uninsured and indigent are two different things. Just because one does not have health insurance does not mean that one is also destitute or unable to pay for their medical care. While this may be the case in many instances, it's not true all of the time and several treatment facilities, like the one this particular Admin. Director works for, have reduced payment plans for uninsured patients who are able to pay for treatment as well as charitable grants for those who can't.

I've found that the best time to research a hospital is when we aren't in need of their services. I operate under the premise that when we need a hospital there may not be time to do the research, to call around and ask questions. In a true emergency though, the best course of action is to get to the *nearest* hospital or call for an ambulance, which may only deliver you to the nearest hospital.

For these reasons, my research begins with that hospital - the one closest to my home. It may not be the hospital I like the best or am the most comfortable with, but in a life or death emergency, I may have no other choice, so it's best to know what I'll be facing in that scenario. I try to keep tabs on at least three local hospitals and make an informed decision about where I'll want myself or my family to go for non-emergency treatments such as ultrasounds and scans, labor and delivery, chemotherapy, etc.

Hospitals are usually fairly busy places, so I save visiting the hospital until the last phase of my research. As usual (and you really should have known this was coming), I start with my computer. I begin by finding the websites of the three nearest hospitals. I scan through their sites to see what types of services they have on-site, the names of the people in charge at the hospital and the names and contact information of the Board of Directors. I compile a file on each hospital so that I have information available more handily later since it's likely I won't like the same hospital for different treatments. For example I may find that one of them is definitely the place I would want to deliver a baby (not that I *want* to deliver any more babies -two is plenty for me, thank you very much!) because of their awesome birthing center, but would rather go into the next county for radiation therapy.

I also look at any FAQ (frequently asked questions) sections that they have, which may answer some of my questions, read any of their on-line forums to see what other people have said about them, check out their blogs or news sections to see what their latest announcements are about. The other thing I want to do is find out if there are any complaints or major lawsuits out against them. There are several websites that track complaints and grade hospitals on certain categories. For example www.HealthGrades.com has a hospital rating section in it. You can buy a comprehensive report on any hospital for about $18. I'm not really into buying reports - there's just so much free information on the Net, but if you are willing to part with it, I'm sure the report has a wealth of information on any hospital you are researching. They also have a free section that will rate your hospital on various different aspects. I checked on my area (northern Virginia) for maternity care. I found out that the closest hospital to me received three stars for maternity care, the hospital in the next county (where my older son was born) also received three stars. The hospital two counties away (the one where my younger son was born) received five stars!

This surprised me because I remember being more impressed by the hospital my first son was born in and I know they've completely remodeled their birthing center since then, so it's still fairly new. So, I clicked on the rating button and found that their grades for maternity care are based on a) the volume of babies they deliver, b) the percentage of complications that they experience, c) the number of infant mortalities they have. Those are pretty important things to consider. I based my experience on whether or not I had a private room and if the nurses answered every blasted page I made to them, etc. Not really a good rating system - kudos to HealthGrades for looking at things I didn't.

Now, to break it down ever further, if you click on the plus sign next to each hospital listed it gives you their statistics on which their grades are based. When I look at the two hospitals I gave birth in, it's easy to see why the second has a much higher grade. First of all, they deliver almost twice the amount of babies as the first, their percentage of complications is about 1.5% less and their newborn survival rate is stated as "best" whereas the first is "as expected" (whatever that means).

You can do this check for any type of treatment at nearly any hospital. It's not concrete evidence of the best hospital, but it gives you something to go on. Having other professionals' opinions is important, but I still like to do some more checking. Some other web sites that have similar ratings systems or hospital report cards are www.qualitycheck.org, www.consumerreports.org and www.healthcarechoices.org,.

The next thing I try to find out is *how* they do business. I start by getting the phone number and calling the information desk. I'll first introduce myself as a "self-pay patient" - they are familiar with that term, which signifies to them that I have no insurance, but that I am educated about the process of medical treatment. It always helps to know the lingo. I'll ask her/him what the hospital policy is on admitting self-pay patients who come in for emergency care (either in an ambulance or on their own). I almost guarantee that they will tell me I'll be admitted just like anyone else, but it will make me feel better to hear it straight from the horse's mouth. It will also send up a big red flag if she/he says otherwise.

Jessica, RN, explained to me that hospitals vary in a very basic way which happens to be a matter of public record. Meaning that you or I can easily tell how each hospital does business and so can determine the likelihood that the hospital will accept you on a self-pay basis.

"As far as admitting noninsured patients," said Jessica, "hospitals have some discretion when it's not a life-threatening situation. Some private hospitals, for example, may choose to turn an uninsured person away."

She went on to explain that private hospitals, which operate through private funding and not through government funds and grants, have a much higher level of independence and can choose how to handle certain situations depending on decisions made by their board. If they see caring for people who don't have health insurance as an income-losing scenario then they may make it a policy to turn those people away unless they have a life-threatening emergency and there are no nearby alternatives.

According to Jessica, in larger metropolitan areas you run a higher risk of being turned down by private hospitals because they aren't willing to run the risk of a financial loss in treating an uninsured patient especially when you could easily make your way to another nearby healthcare facility that will accept you.

In more rural areas where hospitals and treatment centers are fewer and farther between you are more apt to be accepted by even private hospitals, especially under emergency circumstances, because they won't want to risk your life by turning you away when other help may be so remote.

There are different ways that a hospital may be set up to do business. They may be privately owned, as I just explained, but they may also be set up as non-profit, not-for-profit or for-profit entities. The differences are mostly in the way their hierarchy is formed, the way they keep records and pay taxes and the way they fund themselves. However, some of that will naturally trickle down into the actual treatment of patients. For the most part, said Jessica, hospitals that are funded by government/tax dollars or are set up as non-profit or not-for-profit organizations will not turn patients away under any circumstance, but it's still best to know these things ahead of time just to be sure.

One way that I know our county hospital admits and treats patients regardless of insurance status, without even bothering to look up what type of hospital it is, is because of a weird experience my accountant had at this particular hospital. He once had a scheduled surgery that was necessary and couldn't be put off any longer. The bad news (aside from what was ailing him) was that it was tax season and he was absolutely swamped with work.

He was admitted and every time the nurses and doctors entered his room they found him frantically working away on his laptop computer. For some reason they interpreted this as him not having any medical insurance or a job with paid leave and that he was so poor that he couldn't really afford the time off of work to have this surgery. Of course the fact that he'd forgotten to bring his insurance card with him didn't do anything to dissuade them from this misinterpretation.

The truth of the matter was that he felt pressured to get more done for his clients during his busiest season and his wife would be bringing their insurance information later on. Nevertheless, they assumed he was a self-pay patient and treated him no differently than any other patient. In fact he had no idea that they'd formed this opinion of him until after the procedure when a financial councilor came to his room to see if they could work out a payment plan for his bill.

When he was telling me this story I quickly responded asking him if he'd gone along and let them believe what they wanted and found a way to negotiate the bill and payments. It would have been a stroke of genius to get them to drop their rates just like that and then submit his insurance information on the way out the door the next day. They were making it really easy for him, unfortunately he hadn't thought of that until later. Anyway, the real point is that they admitted him and performed surgery on him all the while thinking he had no medical insurance and never once treated him with contempt or give him anything but quality care.

Assuming any hospital will admit a self-pay patient with no problem, next I'll want to know about any other hospital policies that may differ for a self-pay patient, hopefully this will cover some questions I may not know to ask. I also want to know what their payment policy is: will they expect to be paid before I leave or will they bill me later? Must I pay in a lump sum or can I work out a payment plan? Another good question to ask is what simple everyday common things do they use for their patients that could easily be supplied by the patient: what I am looking for here is a list of items I could bring with me if anyone in my family seeks treatment at this hospital. The bill will be smaller if we provide our own Tylenol or Excedrin, cotton swabs, toilet paper, bandages, etc. Lastly, I want to know if I can arrange for an administrator to give me a personal tour of the hospital.

When I'm there, I'll ask all of the same questions again. It may seem redundant, but I'm looking for inconsistencies. If any of the information I get in person is different than what I got over the phone, I'll stop and ask if there's a reason I heard differently on another day and see if the administrator is willing to check it out and tell me definitively which is the correct information. I'm looking for good information, but I'm also trying to get a feel for the facility: does the place look clean and well-maintained, do the staff look professional and friendly, do the staff seem knowledgeable, does it look crowded or does there appear to be ample room and staff for the number of patients present? If anything makes me feel uneasy, including feeling like I'm not getting straight information that could lead to unpleasant "surprises" should I bring a loved one here for any type of treatment, I'm not going to waste much time there, unless this is the service hospital for my residence. In which case, I'll probably waste more time there trying to get to the bottom of things.

This may seem a bit invasive or overtly bold, but after the tour is over and I've said goodbye to the guide, I will sometimes make my way to a waiting room and see if I can strike up a conversation with some of the "waiters". I steer clear of ones who seem to be traumatized, crying or in shock - they may be going through some ghastly ordeal with a loved one and don't need an impromptu interview. If I find someone suitable, I'll ask (very carefully and politely) what treatment they are there for and what type of service and care they've received. Have they been treated there before and what is their opinion of the place and the people working there.

If you're feeling shy I would suggest starting in the maternity ward's waiting room - the people there are typically very happy as many of them are awaiting new arrivals and won't mind telling a stranger about their experiences.

I once did a story for a local newspaper on the opening of a nearby hospital's new birthing center. It was a great excuse for wandering around and talking to people: doctors, nurses, administrators, patients, etc. Everyone was very friendly, especially the closer I got to the maternity ward. The truth of the matter is that nearly everyone likes to talk to reporters if they think they might see their name in print - unless they have something to hide! So I generally try to gauge the reactions I get when I introduce myself to staff members as a writer. If people smile and gush forth with information or even just strictly answer my questions in a straightforward manner I know things are generally good. It's when people hesitate to speak, tell me they'll have to look into it and get back to me or refer me to PR people or higher-ranking administrators that I start to feel uncomfortable.

I would also make an effort to stop at the financial services office. These are the people I'll be dealing with when it comes time to paying the piper. I will ask about their financial aid programs, payment plans, etc. I'll ask if they have a list of their "standard" pricing, perhaps some of the routine things they do have a set price, like a paperwork fee, an admittance fee, and other fees for things like taking blood pressure, urine tests, etc. I'll also be sure to ask what complementary services they may have throughout the year. Some have traveling vans that perform free services or health fairs where small scans or screenings or treatments take place.

As I compile my research I start comparing the information from one hospital to that of the others. Did any of them make me feel uncomfortable or scared in any way? Did one of them give me a complete list of prices for their standardized treatments? Was one of them fairly dirty and overcrowded? Did one of them receive five stars on several categories in their report card? Sometimes one hospital in particular appears better than the others in every way or that they each shine in different aspects. The great thing is that I don't have to choose just one and I don't have to choose right now, but having that information will make it easier to choose when the time comes and I or a member of my family are in need of treatment. We may be too grief-stricken or in shock to do the research after a difficult diagnosis, but we'll have all of the information handy to make a good decision about where to go for treatment.

One thing that had never entered my mind that Jessica brought to my attention is that there are a large number of teaching hospitals around the country. These are mostly hospitals that are run in conjunction with a nearby university so that med students have a facility in which to practice their newly learned skills under supervision.

This is an excellent alternative and according to Jessica, may be one that not only admits noninsured patients, but one that welcomes them. They tend to provide services at a much lower rate, or even for free, just for the sake of having enough patients to accommodate their students. She recommends checking nearby universities to see if they offer medical degrees and if so at which facilities their students can be found. Then talk to those facilities to see what their policies are as far as treating patients with no insurance and pricing their services.

I know it seems like a lot of time and effort to do this much research about your hospital options. Truth is: it IS. There's no getting around it - it WILL take a lot of your time and much effort. The good news is that you don't have to do it all at once. Feel free to spread it out and tackle it in phases. It isn't absolutely necessary and you may opt not to go through this research phase. A friend of mine has even told me she can't see many people going through the amount of time and trouble I do to find a good doctor, yet alone a hospital. She may be right. BUT... it's something that can never be considered a waste of time. It really does bring peace of mind and make your life easier in the long run.

I hope you and I never have to find out if all of the research on hospitals was worth the time and effort, but I'm more than certain that if the day comes when one of us in need of a hospital we'll instantly be grateful that we have that information. Sadly, many people find out about substandard practices at hospitals the hard way. The hard way isn't the way you want to find out if you're at the right care center.

The next time I encounter a hospital will likely be when myself or someone I love is in need of care and this experience will be on a whole new level. As a patient we'll be able to see firsthand if they measure up to all of the information and feelings and thoughts I've gathered about this place during my research phase.

I don't know if you've ever delivered a baby, but one of the first things they'll teach you in your birthing class is that in your third trimester you should have a suitcase packed with everything you want to have with you during your hospital stay ready by the door so that when

THE time comes, you won't have to think about it, just grab it and go. I believe in having a similar plan for any hospital visit. Of course, I'm not going to pack right now, but should someone in my immediate family need treatment I'll want to remember to bring those common, everyday items that will help decrease our bill and make our patient more comfortable. Here's a basic list of items I will likely take with me - for personal effects and for medical reasons:

A) Paperwork/Documents: medical documents, research, reports, etc. of the diagnosis received, treatment we are there for, any health insurance cards (catastrophic health insurance, high deductible insurance, etc.), ID - driver's license, social security card, phone numbers for anyone we may need to contact (including our attorney -just in case, no pun intended), a list of any medications the patient is taking.

B) A change of clothes, bathrobe, pajamas, slippers, eyeglasses and some toiletries.

C) Loose change for the vending machines, newspapers, magazines and perhaps parking meters.

D) Something to cure boredom: a book, magazines, crossword puzzles, knitting, electronics (if allowed by the hospital).

E) Pad and pen - to take notes about anything the doctor or other staff tells us or to jot down questions we want to remember to ask.

F) Regular medications - I'll want to be sure to let the nursing staff know about the patient's regular medications and that we are providing our own - they are not to administer those medications to the patient.

G) First Aid and Conveniences - it may seem really silly, but some hospitals charge for things like toilet paper, tissues, bath towel usage and laundering, cotton swabs and balls, band aids. If you bring these items with you and use only your own, you can demand that they be stricken from your bill.

H) Most important: Trusted Soul. I believe that every patient should have one of these! Someone the patient trusts implicitly to stay with them and look out for them during their stay. That person should keep notes on every procedure, treatment, medication and service provided to the patient while in the hospital. They should also speak up for the patient if the staff is doing something they specifically didn't want - like administering medications they'd said they would not take, ignoring the patient's pages and concerns, and just generally looking out for the patient and being their liaison to the hospital staff.

The last encounter we'll have with the hospital might possibly be the scariest yet - payment. According to Peter Davidson for Bankrate.com you should "never pay your bill before leaving the hospital -- even if you're told it's required". Although he didn't say what to do if the hospital requires it, try to figure out another way. Now, luckily (I say as I knock on my wooden desk) my family has not yet encountered a hospital visit or emergency care, but I know there are definitely things I would do if faced with a hospital bill. At the very least

I'll want to review the invoice and make sure it's accurate before paying even one red cent, regardless of any pay-before-you-leave policies. I'll plop right down in the waiting room and hash through it before I leave if I have to. It's much more difficult to get people to negotiate their invoices after you've made a payment, even if it's just a partial payment.

"Before getting treatment at a hospital," suggests the Admin. Director, "ask for an estimate of what the total charges are likely to be; they should be able to provide that and you should be able to negotiate down. It certainly won't hurt to try."

If I can, I'll persuade them to bill me later. If not, I'll do my best to make arrangements to make just a small payment on the way out (perhaps 10 percent of the bill, or a fixed price like $200) and the balance later. If I'm met with Nurse Ratchet's desk twin I'll ask to speak to the chief of staff (refer to him or her by name - it should be in your research). Name dropping can be such a fabulous thing - just the mere fact that I'd know the name of this mighty person may be enough to win the argument for me, but if I do actually have to go through the chief, I'll be sure to keep composed and make my case carefully. Note to self: NEVER imply that you KNOW the person who's name you're dropping (unless you actually do) because if you have to meet face-to-face with that person, that will be a hard act to sell.

"Estimates on hospital overcharges run up to $10 billion a year, with an average of $1300 per hospital stay. Other experts say overcharges make up approximately 5% of hospital bills," claims Davidson.

My favorite part of his article, though, was when he quoted a medical billing advocate who said she'd seen a hospital bill with a $129 charge for a mucous recovery system only to find out that her client was being billed for a box of tissues.

Davidson and his sources say that some hospitals bill erroneously deliberately and some do it by accident (like his example that a man's hip replacement surgery bill included newborn blood tests and a crib mobile), but that almost all hospital bills are fraught with errors hiding in coded language, making it very difficult for regular Joes like us to interpret and understand, yet alone pick apart and argue over.

What I'll want to see is an itemized bill, where each and every penny is accounted for - no lump sums. If you get a lump sum invoice, ask the hospital, or billing agent, to give you a break out of the costs in writing.

The next thing I'll want to do is review each and every line of that invoice with a hospital administrator (in person or on the phone) and find out what it all means. The next thing is to start striking things off of the invoice and having the charges reduced. That example of a $129 mucous recovery system - even knowing it's a box of tissues you know it's not reasonable to charge that much. If I see a $129 box of tissues on my bill, I plan to tell them, in no uncertain terms that I won't pay more than $5 for it, even though that's still more than it's worth. And I'll be doing that for every single line.

To help you visualize this better I've included some sample hospital bills I found on the Internet. There are three, which you can see for yourself in Appendices B, C and D. In example bill 1 (Appendix B) you will see that it seems very straightforward and simple - only 2 lines and a total. On second glance, though, you may notice that the second line is the same as the first, only it says "multiple" after "complete ultrasound". What does that mean? It could mean that more than one ultrasound was taken, but it could also mean that they made more than one hardcopy of the ultrasound results.

If there were more than one ultrasound taken, why are they priced differently? I would ask for them to both be $200 (or less). If "multiple" means they made a copy of the original, then I would ask what type of copy was made. Did they photo copy it? Because you can do that at Kinko's for under 10 cents. Did they make another copy on their special film? That could be worth more, but probably not more than $50. If this were my bill I'd want to find out what they are willing to do, and if I'm still not satisfied, I'd start calling around to other hospitals. What do they charge for ultrasounds? If I'd gotten an estimate before the ultrasound was taken and now they are charging more, I'd be sure to tell them that I'd received a quote for the scan ahead of time and that they need to honor it.

In example number 2 (Appendix C), I don't even know where to begin. My first question is: What the heck is "8C"? and why does it cost almost $2500? My next question would be: What is CSD, General Chemistry and Pharmacy? It seems that this hospital is really good at trying to hide their fees in unexplained invoice lines. Not only that, but look at the way the bill is laid out. What you see first is the amount due - it's $50. You're thinking, wow, I only owe $50 for such a huge treatment, that's not bad. But what you should be noticing is that the bill actually comes to $8,320.05 and that you owe $200 - the $50 is just their minimum payment requirement. In this case, Trigon BlueCross BlueShield insurance is paying most of the bill, which is great, but even so I would still question everything. I'd start by calling the hospital and getting them to decode each line and tell me what they include and then, just as before, start striking things from the list.

If I had to guess, I'd say that 8C is a room number and that the hospital has a standard rate for that room that they multiplied by the number of days it was occupied. If this were my bill I'd call and find out what the room rate is and what it includes. If it includes items we didn't use, I'd have them take it off. The idea is to deduct as much as possible. Even if I can get them to just deduct the amount the insurance company pays, it still benefits me (and the rest of us, in general). The less money insurance companies have to pay out, the lower premiums will be, in theory anyway. As a self-pay patient however, every penny I knock off my bill is a penny I get to keep in my pocket.

This bill really looks like a sneaky one to me - there's just so little explanation for such a large amount and yet they try to make it look like it's a small bill with your itty-bitty "Amount Due" showing just $50. I would really pick this one apart and whittle it down.

Now example bill 3 (Appendix D) truly confounds me. There is so much information and explanation that came with this bill that it appears almost straightforward...almost.

The great thing about this bill is that everything is laid out and explained in plain site. It comes with a summary and a second page which is an itemized explanation of the charges.

One of the pitfalls of this bill, however, is the vagueness of the itemization. Take the first line for example: Room and Care. The room, I get - hospitals will generally have a daily room rate that they charge for in-patient care, but how much of that $6273 is for room and how much for "care" - and what exactly is included in care?

Many of the other lines on that itemized list are just as ambiguous. If this were my bill I'd want a better definition of "pharmacy", "central services/supplies", "operating room services" and many others. It's fairly easy to assume that this person was in the hospital for four days; the first page of the bill dates services rendered on 2/1 and a discharge date of 2/4, and that he had some type of surgery, needed medications and an EKG. The rest, though, is a bit fuzzy. I'd want the hospital to really spell out for me what they did, step by step, and how much I'm being charged for each specific service.

The second thing that glares at me from this bill is that this particular four-day stay cost over $27,000 - that's a LOT of money. Luckily, this John Doe has insurance that appears to have negotiated away $23,000 of this bill. Keep that in mind when you're negotiating your own hospital bills: insurance companies can make 85 percent of a bill disappear, so you should aim for getting a great deal, too.

You may not be able to haggle your way down to just 15 percent of your bill, like an insurance company can, though. Think of HMO's a little like Costco: huge volumes of merchandise and large masses of members gives them a tremendous bargaining chip when it comes to purchases. This is how they are able to offer such large quantities of products for cheaper prices. Insurance companies, likewise, have an enormous customer base and do extraordinary volumes of business with any given medical entity, so they are able to demand big discounts. You, on the other hand, are a single customer who (hopefully) won't be doing an awful lot of business with your hospital, so you won't have the ability to command the same sort of discount as an HMO. But that shouldn't stop you from trying.

One thing you might want to try is to get a hospital administrator to tell you what a major HMO's negotiated rates are for your particular bill. That will give you a good idea of the discount they are getting and then use that information to persuade the hospital to cut their rates for you, as well. If the HMO is slashing 85 percent, maybe the hospital would be willing to give you 75 percent off?

Again, looking at sample bill #3: The insurance company is also taking financial responsibility for approximately $4000 of the remaining balance and Doe's personal payment of $40 is due.

Doe got a heck of a deal here - $27,000 in medical services for $40. That doesn't get him out of going over this bill with a fine-tooth comb, though.

One of the biggest problems with health insurance is that feeling of non-accountability. You start becoming complacent about medical billing and think that it's up the HMO to deal with it all and sort it out. I know I felt that way when my family had insurance. I never really looked into my medical bills. So long as no one asked me to pay more than my pre-defined co-payments I was happy. But the reality is that YOU are responsible for all of your medical bills and, insurance or not, you really need to take it seriously. Don't wait for what I call "The Fallout" - where you don't even think about your medical bills until after your insurance negotiates their allowable fees, pays there share and then the rest falls out into your lap for you to pay. Never again will I be so negligent. Since ditching health insurance I have reviewed and negotiated every medical bill incurred on behalf of each of my family members. I don't always get the bills reduced, but I do always make sure the bill is broken out and understandable.

Nearly all hospitals (in fact, I would say ALL, except that I know someone out there will find that *one* dinky exception) have entire billing and financial departments whose sole responsibility is to prepare medical bills and to deal with patients and their financial problems. A hospital near me has financial counselors who are set up to work with patients who have difficulty in paying their medical bills. I know several people who've been through these trials and tribulations with hospitals and I know that when (hopefully never) it's my turn to deal with them I'll be slashing the hash until they just won't go any lower. And after negotiating a bill with the regular hospital billing staff to ensure that it's accurate and as low as it can be (for now) I'll be making an appointment with a hospital financial counselor. The purpose of this meeting will be to plead my case or *bargain for our lives.* I'll want to impress upon this person how desperately poor we are and what a hardship the hospital bill will put on my financial wellbeing and that of my family.

I will be fully prepared when I enter this meeting: I will bring with me supporting documents like tax returns, financial statements (since we're self-employed), bank statements, etc. I'm not trying to lie to this person or fool her. I may exaggerate a bit, carefully though. What I'll want to convey to this person is that I have little ability to pay the bill in full, since I'm self-employed and uninsured and will have to pay it all out-of-pocket. I'll want to win this person over and have her on my side so that she really feels for me, likes me and genuinely wants to help me. While it may well be her job to get people to make payments to the hospital who has employed her, I know that any amount she can take off my bill isn't coming directly out of her pocket. I'll want to use that to my advantage and see if I can't get her to sympathize and identify with my financial situation more than the hospital's. After all, what's a couple thousand dollars less to a big institution like the hospital? Not much, but it's quite a tidy sum to me and my family - and probably would be to her, personally, as well.

(You might notice that I keep referring to this hospital financial counselor as *she*. That's because, in my opinion, it's easier to negotiate with women. Women, in general, have a more difficult time separating their emotions from business and therefore it will likely be easier to get a woman to sympathize with you and want to help your situation.)

I would sit down in this person's office, wearing a nice outfit no jeans and T-shirt, but nothing fancy or expensive either, something modest. I would explain that I am there seeking help about my invoice because my husband and I are both self-employed with little income and no health insurance. I would mention the typical amount of income we earn and show her through our spreadsheets or tax returns and indicate to her the amount of expenses we encounter throughout a year while maintaining our family of ourselves and our two growing boys (emphasis on growing - as in constantly needing new clothing, food and other supplies).

Anyway, I would definitely emphasize the double self-employment status of my family and the growing boys and back it up with my documents. You may ask if she has kids and say something like, "Oh, well then you know what it's like to keep up with feeding and clothing the little rascals." Or if not "Oh, then you have no idea how many sacks of groceries a tween-age boy can eat before they even make it to your kitchen counter!" Keep it light and friendly.

The last thing you want to do is go into such a meeting with a chip on your shoulder. Remember, you are there basically asking for a favor. If you behave in an angry or self-righteous manner, what incentive does the staff member have to help you? While it may be her job to help you out, she certainly isn't going to bend over backwards for someone who's yelling, condescending, arrogant, cursing or aggressive towards her.

I want her to know that I am aware that HMOs negotiate medical costs and that often hospital charges go above their "caps". I also want her to know that even though I don't have an HMO negotiating for me, I'll be doing so for myself and are seeking her help to lower the bill to what an insurance company would allow, or perhaps she can allow a blanket discount over the entire bill if I agree to pay it all at once or in two equal payments. As with anything - cash talks. Since I would have already negotiated the bill prior to this meeting, hopefully it's already at a reasonable level and this further discount will really be a bonus, but if not, I'll let her know how devastating this bill is. I wouldn't offer a monthly payment until we've settled the bottom line. They may be willing to accept $100 monthly payments for 10 years in order to collect their $12,000 while I have my mind set on getting the bill down to $9,000.

That would actually be a discount of 25 percent. I usually find a direct route is the best way to go, so I may just flat out ask, "Is there anyway you can discount the bill since I'm a self-pay patient - I just don't have the means to pay such a large bill like the major medical insurance companies do?" I might tell her that we could handle $8,000 with only a fair amount of difficulty, but $12,000 would absolutely devastate my family's financial well-being. Perhaps we'll have to settle for somewhere in the middle, but hopefully we'll be able to negotiate something lower than the previously negotiated bill.

Once we've agreed on a bottom line I'll ask what type of payment options are available. Can I make $100 monthly payments? I believe most hospitals will be able to grant a monthly payment plan, but if the minimum monthly payment is more than we can afford, I'll want to tell them up front that we just won't be able to pay that amount per month and still keep up with our mortgage, utilities, groceries, etc. and see if they can either further discount our bill or reduce the monthly payments.

If, for some reason, they want all of their money at once and won't grant a payment plan, I will need to look into another method of payment, unless by some miracle of faith we do have the cash on hand. I would start with a personal loan, either from a local bank, or more preferable, from a good friend or family member. I would never even consider using a credit card. First of all, because we hate them and no longer have any, but also because if you default on your monthly payments to them you could wind up with a much larger balance owed to them than your original hospital bill.

Hospitals are businesses and they are trying to make money, so I know I'm not going to get something for nothing from them. On the other hand they are doing fabulous work helping people, me included, and that there is great value in their work. When negotiating anything I try to respect the other person or business and know that even if they are greedy or underhanded, they have something that is of value to me, otherwise I wouldn't be negotiating with them. I'll do my best to work with them and get the most out of it that I can, but it can be disheartening if I can't get what I want, or even close. But there are always other options. I've never tried it with a hospital, but there's always the barter route - see if they need my help for a while to pay off my debt. The more options I can put before them of work I could do for them the harder it will be for them to prove to a court that I was unwilling to pay off my account, should it come to that.

And as always, I'll be documenting everything: a log of my phone conversations and personal meetings; with whom I spoke and when, what was said, what was offered, agreed to, denied, etc. If I can keep in close communications with the hospital, chances are, I truly believe, the two of us will be able to work something out eventually.

All billing aside, there is one more concept about hospitals and medical doctors in general that warrants consideration. What to do when there's nothing else they can do for your health and well-being.

According to Jessica, RN, there's no stopping a doctor from trying to "cure" a sick person. This sounds like a really good quality in a medical professional, but what she means is that if you have a life threatening disease doctors tend to operate and operate and suggest treatment after treatment even after it's apparent that they won't a) ever be able to rid you of the disease, b) be able to extend your life or c) be able to improve the quality of the life you have left.

"I don't know what's wrong with us in America," said Jessica, "we are one of the only nations that refuses to talk about death and to help people prepare for it."

Maybe it's the same element that keeps doctors from making declarative statements to patients and their families about their treatments or lengths of time for recovery or lifespan, but something keeps them from just saying the awful truth about end-of-life matters.

"They should be able to look their patients and their patients' families in the eye and say, 'I am so sorry for what is happening to you. Truly, it sucks. I think you probably have six months left and I think you would be better served by enjoying the time you have left with your family and tying up loose ends.' and then introducing them to Hospice or some other end-of-life organization that can help them make the most of the time they have left, comfortably."

It really is a shame to see people who are already suffering go through procedure after procedure only to spend the rest of their days in a hospital in vain. There needs to come a point where it's ok to just go home and be with the people you love. Of course I would never tell anyone not to fight for their life, but if there's no quality to your life, then why shouldn't the medical profession be on your side enough to honestly tell you to go home and be with family and friends. Even if you live twice as long as anyone would expect you to, at least you'll have the satisfaction of using that time to your advantage.

I don't know what type of reaction you might get, but if you feel you're in that type of a situation - where you have a fatal diagnosis and modern medicine cannot offer you a cure, ask your doctor to open up and be honest with you. Ask him or her to respect your life enough to give you time with your loved ones - enough time to really enjoy them while you can and to not waste your final days suffering through surgeries and living in treatment facilities.

For those of you unfamiliar with Hospice, they are a not-forprofit organization that will provide medical and personal assistance to patients, who's doctor has referred them with a diagnosis of six months or less to live, and their families. They are particularly skilled at making sure the patient has everything they need to be comfortable at home, including pain management.

In addition to the medical help they provide, Hospice can also assist with emotional and other issues that may arise while the patient and their family are dealing with a life-limiting illness. If the patient outlives the doctor's initial diagnosis Hospice will still offer assistance if, after the six month period is over, the patient's doctor still believes that person is terminally ill.

They are a tremendous asset to anyone dealing with a life-limiting illness and will do their best to make sure everyone involved is cared for. Once the patient succumbs to their illness, Hospice stays in place and offers counseling and assistance to the family for up to one year.

Hospice is covered for patients who have Medicare or Medicaid. Their web site (www.HospiceFoundation.org) also noted that several independent health insurance companies will partially cover Hospice services. They made no mention about costs for patients with no health insurance, but I'm sure with the proper diagnosis they would be able to help on some level, although the financial aspect of it would need to be discussed ahead of time.

Chapter 9: Dealing with Disaster

The first rule in surviving and thriving in any calamitous situation: don't panic! The same rule applies to medical crises. If you keep your wits about you, you will have a much better chance of making good decisions.

One of the realizations that my family has come to since dropping our health insurance is that any medical care we receive above and beyond annual checkups is an unexpected expense. And unexpected expenses can throw our entire monthly or annual budget out of whack.

We try to be smart with our money. Several times I've recalculated our budget (usually after a new expense that I'd overlooked or was unaware of rears its ugly head and sends me in a tizzy) to try to come up with an improved plan so that when unexpected expenses come to call we're better prepared and able to handle the setback more efficiently. My initial plan was to use about half of what we were spending on health insurance to help pay our monthly bills and take the other half and stash it into savings as an emergency fund.

This is what I was hoping would happen:

We were paying about $600 per month on health insurance premiums.

After cancelling our policy I would use $300 of that $600 on bills and stash the other $300 in an interest-bearing savings account, which at that time was earning about a 3 percent APR.

In just one year, we would have set aside $3600 in our nest egg and earned an additional $60 in interest. While that's not a whole lot, if we keep doing this steadily and hopefully have a buffer of several years before any devastating medical needs arise this number would keep compounding.

Imagine if we can do this for five or 10 years or, God-willing, even longer. When disaster strikes, we'll have a tidy sum of money set aside for our healthcare and when unexpected medical expenses arise we won't feel so overwhelmed and panic-stricken.

Unfortunately, our monthly obligations proved too burdensome for us to keep up this plan. We wound up needing every penny we'd saved by cancelling our health insurance to catch up on bills we'd fallen behind on and to sustain us through some very lean years. We tried not to worry, though, we knew there were still ways to cope with traumatic and expensive medical news.

One great way to save for medical expenses is through FSAs (Flexible Spending Accounts). These accounts are typically set up by employers and if you enroll you can have money set aside directly from your paycheck into an FSA, pretax. Now, you may not be earning interest like in a bank savings account, but you are spending pretax dollars -

money that is not taxed by the IRS or your state as income tax, which might be a greater advantage than three percent or whatever your bank is offering.

An example of FSA savings found on Wikipedia is as follows:

Scenario 1 -No FSA Account, Spending Out-of-Pocket
                  Income = $50,000
                  Tax Rate = 40% (on $50,000)
                  Medical Expenses = $2000
                  Net Income = $28,000

Scenario 2 -FSA Savings for Healthcare
                  Income = $50,000
                  Tax Rate = 40% (on $48,000)
                  Medical Expenses = $2000
                  Net Income = $28,800

You can see by this example that by saving your money in an FSA you also save $800 on your tax return. By letting your employer pay you $2000 less over the year and using that money to pay for medical expenses you get to pay Uncle Sam $800 less because that $2000 of your income that was set aside pretax.

There are drawbacks to FSAs, though. First of all, you have to be employed. Second, you have to be employed by a company that offers such a plan. Third you need to calculate your FSA contributions carefully, if you don't use all of the money you had set aside in an FSA within your company's defined plan year, you could be responsible for paying taxes on the portion left over and if you don't file for an FSA refund quickly enough you may never see that money again, even though you are now obligated to pay taxes on it.

Also, there are limits to what you can use FSA funds for. They essentially were set up to help people pay out-of-pocket medical expenses that insurance doesn't cover. You can pay your doctor's visit co-payments, your portion of doctor's fees over and above what the insurance pays, prescription drugs, even childcare, elderly care, etc. If you plan to sign up for an FSA be sure to talk to your company about the rules and restrictions of their plan, i.e. in some instances you have to be married to a working spouse in order to use an FSA. Also be sure to get a copy of their cafeteria plan - the approved expenses for your FSA.

While FSA's are great, for self-employed people they're pretty much a mirage. For those of us who are working for ourselves (who are the greatest bosses on earth, by the way) we have to come up with other ways of saving and preparing for medical expenses.

Even after you've gotten a devastating diagnosis or been in an aggravating accident, it's not too late to shop for health insurance to help you defray the costs of your care.

Many insurance companies will still accept patients into their health plans even with preexisting conditions, although they may impose a defined waiting period until they begin to cover a preexisting condition, typically 12 months. While this may seem an interminable period of time, during which bills are mounting, it is still better to have coverage down the road, because chances are that whatever has changed in your health will need further treatments, surgeries and/or checkups that may occur after that waiting period.

It is also possible to find health insurance policies that do not have a waiting period for existing or preexisting conditions. They are rare, but they are out there and if you find one, my advice -snatch it up!

In many cases, insurance plans that are willing to sign on people with preexisting conditions (with or without the waiting period) will only offer limited coverage. Typically they will have either a discount plan, whereby expenses are all covered up to a certain percentage of the bill and the patient is responsible for the remainder of the cost or they will cover medical expenses up to a certain annual or lifetime maximum.

According to MedHealthInsurance, several states have programs in place called "high risk insurance pools" which will provide coverage to individuals with preexisting conditions. While these plans practically guarantee insurance coverage for people with high risk diseases and conditions (like cancer, diabetes, fibromyalgia, depression, drug abuse, etc.) who may not be able to get into other health plans, they tend to be very expensive and may also have a waiting period and/or only offer limited coverage. When it comes right down to it, though, an expensive health care plan may still be more affordable than debilitating medical bills.

At present every state in the U.S. also offers guaranteed health plans known as Mini-Meds. These are designed to cover uninsured Americans who can afford health insurance but are not part of any group or are considered "uninsurable" because of existing or preexisting medical conditions that will most likely need constant and/or extremely expensive medical care. These, too, are limited health plans and while no one can be turned down, they only cover a limited amount of care. This plan can still be beneficial, offering to cover all or some of a policy-holder's medical expenses but is also set up to protect the insurance companies by limiting their liability in return for offering insurance to people who would not, otherwise, have any at all.

To find a list of Mini-Med plans in any state, log onto the Internet and go to http://www.minimeds.com/. Near the bottom of the page, click on the pull-down menu arrow and choose your state of residence and click on "search".

Additionally, states offer Medicare plans that can cover a woman AFTER she becomes pregnant. In Chapter 2, I addressed state plans that cover children under Medicare so that you can have insurance for free for your children. The same plans offer free medical coverage for pregnant women to ensure they have healthy babies. If pregnancy is your preexisting condition, this is a fantastic (and did I mention FREE?) way to go. Although, like the free children's insurance, there is a household income maximum requirement. That amount may vary from state to state, but essentially if your family earns around $40,000 or less annually you may be able to qualify.

The state plans for pregnant women will cover everything from prenatal care to labor and delivery and recovery at no cost. There may be very nominal co-payments for doctor's visits (something like $5 or less). The only drawbacks to these plans is the limited number of doctor's who accept this plan, although in my state (Virginia) the plan comes with a booklet or on-line directory to help you locate a doctor near you who will accept the state's medical plan and which hospitals will do likewise.

No offense - I love my children dearly, but I'm hoping I'll never qualify for this plan. And it's likely that when the economy, and therefore our incomes, improve, my children won't qualify for the state's free medical insurance programs either. Since we've been dealing with life without health insurance for several years now already, I'm not worried. I know that there are many options still available and I'm keeping all of my research handy.

Of course, I'm still hoping that we'll need nothing more than a good savings account to keep us in the clear with unexpected medical expenses, but it always makes me feel better to know what's out there and where I'd want to turn first if/when the time comes.

Should a medical disaster strike my family, in addition to working out some sort of insurance or payment plan, I'll want to head back to my research to review the doctor and hospital information I've compiled. While a medical emergency may take us to the nearest healthcare facility due to the nature of the ailment or accident, we may have other options and choices to make.

Of course we won't want to move an unstable or intensive care patient to a new location, but we may want to consider finding out if a less seriously injured family member would be receiving better care or equal care at a less expensive facility. Rest assured, I'll be going over my research and notes with a fine-tooth comb to make sure my family member is at the proper facility, receiving care from a trusted doctor. I'll also be looking to see where we'll want to go for follow-up care and treatments.

There are also alternative treatment facilities designed to care for people in certain situations that I'll want to look into. In my neck of the woods alone I can think of, off the top of my head, at least five different hospitals, a couple of cancer centers, and Hospice care.

Hospice is a fabulous organization that has many locations across the United States and their goal is to help patients facing a diagnosis of six months or less of life left for absolutely no cost. They aid in having end-of-life patients released from hospitals and relocated to care facilities or to the patient's home and help take care of everything from medications and meals to grief therapy and family needs. To locate a Hospice near you, log onto www.hospicenet.org and under "Services" click on "Find a Local Hospice", or you can email them at info@hospicenet.org.

It's also possible to get relief from organizations and individuals in your own community. Many people feel very strongly (especially in tight knit communities) about helping others in their immediate area. Schools, houses of worship, clubs and businesses all routinely set up fundraisers and collections for people in need in their own community. Don't be too proud to ask for help when you need it, many of them would be more than happy to lend a hand, financially or physically.

I can't tell you the number of times my children's school has sent home notices about a fellow student whose family is facing a crisis and asking for help (all too often, I'm afraid) and the response is usually overwhelming. Last year we found out about two children in the school who were diagnosed with Leukemia and this year we've had two families who have lost their homes to fires. It always makes me so proud to walk into the school and see the humongous piles of donations for the families who have lost their homes and the inboxes overflowing with checks to help with family bills and medical expenses.

Another good venue is the government. You may constantly be asking yourself, "What have they done for me lately?" But the truth of the matter is local representatives pride themselves on "keeping their finger on the pulse" of their home communities. Even if they can't get you off the hook for your medical expenses, chances are they know people who can help or organizations who can alleviate the crisis. Write or call the state senate representative for your district, the mayor of the town you're in, the governor of your state, the representatives and delegates for your state in the federal Congress and anyone else you can think of who has been elected to serve you. Heck, call the school board - it can't hurt.

The fact of the matter is that the more you look into these plans now, the better prepared you will be should something happen to you or a loved one. I'm especially proud to have all of this information readily available because I know that if it's me who is ailing, possibly dying, my family won't have to worry about making the right decision. I've taken the time to do the research for them and all they have to do is read through it to know where to turn to and how to get me the best help available. The last thing I want to do if I'm unable to be active in my family is to burden them with making decisions about my care. Having a plan and knowing what options are available is a great way to help alleviate the stress you or your family will be feeling during such a traumatic time.

Chapter 10: Take it With You When You Go

Admittedly, I am a paperwork freak. When you hear the expression "paperless society" it is obviously spoken by someone who has never met me...or seen my office. I'm talking paper, paper everywhere. I print out the emails I think I may need to reference later, I print hard copies of every article I write, I print out homework assignments and study guides from my children's school's web site. I keep copies of all of my bills and confirmations of on-line payments. It just never ends.

I try to be organized about it, so that it doesn't consume me or my home. I have dozens of 3-ring binders in which I sort and organize my papers by category. I have one for utility bills, payments and info, one for government taxes and paperwork, one for bank statements, etc. But I must say one of the most important binders I keep close tabs on is the one labeled "Family Health".

In this binder I keep five sections; one for each of the four members of my family and even one for the dog. In each section is every bill, invoice, information sheet, X-ray, diagnosis, etc. that I have ever gotten at any doctor's office, in the mail or print-out from computer research.

I find it so important to keep all of this information, even though some of it is a decade or more old because health is accumulative. You just never know what might happen. What if my child contracts a disease that I thought he had been inoculated against as an infant? Besides obviously needing to fix the problem, I'll want to reference the paperwork the doctor gave me that day to see if I was mistaken or if the doctor had some fault in the matter.

There are so many minor and important issues that we face with our health that may not become a concern until years down the line. And when that day comes I'll want to have all of the information needed to get to the crux of the matter.

This binder can serve as evidence of neglectful care or billing on the part of a doctor, but it can also provide an important health history for each member of my family.

Some of the health-related paperwork I'm keeping in my binder was given to me voluntarily by our healthcare providers, but some of it I had to request. I try to remember to ask for a copy of all documentation, forms, X-rays, etc. at every visit any of us have with any type of healthcare provider. It's usually no big deal and I've never had anyone turn me down. By the time I get up to the receptionist to pay the bill I simply ask if she can make me a photocopy of any papers going into my file resulting from my visit. Since it's typically just one or two copies, they don't mind.

I must admit, though, that I learned to do this the hard way. Remember that doctor I said I'd been seeing since I was thirteen years old? Well, by the time I was ready to leave and find a new doctor, I'd been at that practice for many, many years. I trusted them implicitly up until then and had sort of formed the habit of leaving all evidence there in the files they kept in their offices.

It wasn't until I found a new doctor that I realized how much paperwork and health history my children and I had accumulated there. When the new doctor asked for our files I had nothing to give her. She advised me to go back to my original physician and request a copy of our files. Which I did. And they politely told me that I would have to pay $30 per file in administrative costs to copy and supply me with all of the paperwork.

At that point, I didn't really know what to do. I was angry that they had the nerve to ask me to pay for my files. I mean, hadn't I been paying for all of those papers all along? Weren't those files really my personal property? Not knowing any better, I complained about the cost, but paid it anyway so that I would have the files in my possession.

Since then I've done a little digging to see what the law says about this scenario. The doctors are required by law to keep on file the originals of all of a patient's health documents for seven years for adults and until the age of 21 for children. They do, in fact, own your medical files and cannot by law just hand them over to you.

Okay, I get that, it sounds reasonable. On the other hand, however, we (the patients) have a right to copies of everything in our medical files, with a few exceptions like psychoanalysis notes and such. Now this, I like. There's a but, though.

BUT (yes, I know, it's a big but) the doctor has the right to charge any patient requesting their medical files a "reasonable fee" according to the rules of HIPAA (Health Insurance Portability and Accountability Act). The U.S. Department of Health and Human Services (www.hhs.gov) says this about medical records in their HIPAA FAQ section:

> Question: If patients request copies of their medical records as permitted by the Privacy Rule, are they required to pay for the copies?
>
> Answer: The Privacy Rule permits the covered entity to impose reasonable, cost-based fees. The fee may include only the cost of copying (including supplies and labor) and postage, if the patient requests that the copy be mailed. If the patient has agreed to receive a summary or explanation of his or her protected health information, the covered entity may also charge a fee for preparation of the summary or explanation. The fee may not include costs associated with searching for and retrieving the requested information.

Call me a rebel, but I do not agree with this - at all. I know, I know, it's the law, so whatcha gonna do? I have two thoughts on getting around this.

First of all, there's the habit I've gotten into now. I ask for a copy of everything going into my file at each visit. My doctor doesn't charge me for this, and I don't imagine any other doctors would either. The fact is that each time I make that request I'm really only asking for a few copies, so it doesn't take up more than one minute of their time and really not much in materials (i.e. paper, ink and toner). Anytime we have X-rays taken (which is most often at the dentist), I just ask if they could make me a photocopy of the film. It's not the best picture, but it's usually adequate for seeing any issues that are evident in the film. If the X-ray is digital, I just ask if they can make me a disc or email it to me so that I have my own copy.

X-rays are particularly handy to keep on hand because if we should need to show it to another healthcare provider I don't have to make a special request later, wait for my doctor to locate the original, make a copy (which sometimes takes longer if another film has to be ordered), and notify me that I can pick it up. All I have to do is take my copy with me at that appointment.

If other files are made at the doctor's office by computer, I will give them the option of printing out a copy to hand to me or emailing it to me later. I prefer a copy in my hand before I go - it's just too likely that the office staff member will get busy and forget to do it later and then it's up to me to keep hounding them until I get it. But sometimes it's just easier to email and I can use my own printing materials to make a hard copy for myself.

The reason that this works, like I said earlier, and that the doctor doesn't charge me is because I am asking for so little each time. Now when I had to ask my doctor for three full files all at once, it immediately looks like a time-consuming project. All of a sudden it's tens, if not hundreds, of photocopies and perhaps an hour of someone's time to make the copies and ready them for me.

While it's essentially the same amount of time and materials going into both requests, it just seems like a less significant job when requested in smaller doses. I, however, still don't believe doctors should be charging patients for copies of medical records. As far as I'm concerned, the doctor may be required to keep originals on file for seven years, but the patient is the true owner of the information. Not only that, but I guarantee you that every time you see your doctor they have an administrative and/or overhead fee woven into the visit charges. It's just standard practice for every business: you always factor your overhead costs into your fees. If not done that way, then a business may break out their charges into overhead or administrative fees, labor/time and materials. Whichever way you slice it, when you think about it, you are paying for the time and office materials of your doctor with every visit. In my mind, this justifies providing patients with copies of their records gratis - either bit by bit at each visit or all at once.

The second idea I had about trying to get your data without having to pay a fee is to offer the doctor a ream of paper and ask if I can stay and use his copier. That way I'm not using up their office supplies or time. I'm not sure how doctors feel about patients using their copying equipment, but if you find a quiet time and won't be too in the way and seem intelligent enough to operate simple machinery I don't see why they'd have a problem. You could always present the argument that you feel it would be an unwise use of the doctor's staff's time and materials to do something as menial as photocopy your files so you are willing to provide the time and materials yourself. It always helps to present your way of doing things as a great favor or benefit to those you are trying to persuade. That way if they feel they have to turn you down they'll think twice about charging you for it since you've been so thoughtful.

Had I had this research to fall back on or had thought it through back then, I definitely would have made this argument with my doctor when his staff charged me $90 for our files. I bet he would have waived this fee - I can be very persuasive when I set my mind to it. Regardless of money, though, it's a good idea to keep medical records on hand.

It's so important for so many reasons. By having our medical records in my possession, I have a complete medical history that I can provide any new healthcare providers to better familiarize them with each member of my family that they will be seeing.

I also find it helpful to keep all of the paperwork in chronological order, for several reasons. First of all, it's just easier to find things when they are stored in date order. It also keeps your records in order by healthcare provider. I know that anything I need to find from the $30 copy-fee doctor will be way in the back circa 1999 or earlier and that anything from our short stint at Kaiser Permanente will be in the era of 2000-2002.

It's also handy to have these records in order in case I or anyone else has to review the file; it gives anyone a better sense of what's happened in our history when it's in order. It's also a better gauge for looking back to see what happened with a certain incident and in what order it happened, should we ever need to go over it with a fine toothed comb because of a medically-related law suit or to locate particular facts and findings should something happen to one of us that we believe is related to something that happened with our health in the past.

Most importantly, though, I believe in keeping these records in my home, in a complete set and organized so that I have a reliable history to look back on. It's all vital information that I don't want to have to rely on the organization and efficiency of others to keep for me. If there's anything I need or want to know about the health history of anyone in my immediately family I know I have the information at my fingertips, I don't have to wait for anyone to get back to me. And being as self-reliant as possible is very important to me.

Chapter 11: Never Bet the Farm

I can't begin to tell you how sad and mad it makes me when I hear stories of how people have lost their homes because of overwhelming medical bills. According to a study by the American Journal of Medicine 62 percent of bankruptcies filed in 2007 cited medical bills as the reason for the hardship. What's even more surprising (or not, depending on your level of cynicism) is that 75 percent of those bankruptcies were filed by individuals or families who had health insurance coverage - at least they did when they first got sick or had an accident.[1]

I am sad for these people and the incredibly bad situation they are in but also mad because I know in most cases, that doesn't need to happen. Naturally, I'm also mad because I know what hounds bill collectors are and they, in my opinion, have no business treating people the way they do.

Trust me when I tell you, I have a lot of experience in dealing with debt collectors. Sadly, when your household finances are fuelled by two self-employment incomes, there are plenty of times when the copper in the coffers just doesn't cover the monthly bills. It's a feast or famine type of lifestyle. The feast periods are wonderful, but few. The famine eras are all too common, disappointing and frequent.

My favorite story (if it's possible to have a favorite with this type of memory) is about our electric company. While building our new home my husband had the electricity turned on several months away from completing the structure so that he could use his power tools without having to run his generators nonstop. I did not know this. And, really, why would I? I wasn't living there yet and since I'm a girl (wink, wink) there wasn't anything I could do on a construction site.

Finally, the house was done and we moved in. About three weeks after we plopped all of our boxes and totes into our new digs I get a call from the electric company. They are threatening to shut off our power and would like to just let us know when that will happen.

I flipped out on this poor woman on the phone, who was, oddly enough, being very nice about the whole situation. Irately (yes, I get immediately irate when companies call me for money and make threats - it's a gut reaction that I refuse to rein in) I told her that we'd only been in the home three weeks and hadn't even received our first

---

[1]

The American Journal of Medicine, Clinical Research Study: Medical Bankruptcy in the United States, 2007: Results of a National Study. © 2009 Elsevier Inc. All rights reserved. The American Journal of Medicine (2009)

bill yet. This was in March. Electra-girl informed me that our power had been turned on in November and not one penny had yet to be paid.

I confirmed with my ever-so-innocent honey that this was indeed. Only, he doesn't pay the bills, I do. So I didn't know there was power and he didn't know I hadn't been getting the bills.

I asked Electra-girl where she was sending the bills. She said they'd been going to our previous house, the address we'd given them when we first informed them of our building project. The thing was, we had to sell the house and move in with my mother-in-law during construction in order to pay for the building materials and our mail was no longer being forwarded. This got me even hotter.

"You mean you've been sending me bills for five months and they've been coming back to the electric company and you couldn't figure out that something was wrong?"

"You mean that at no time in that period you ever once thought to send the bill to the same place you were sending the electricity, or to call me on the phone before now?"

"You mean that now that you're fed up with me you're going to physically send someone to my house to shut off power, but at no time in that five-month period you thought to send someone out to see why we weren't getting or paying our bills?"

At this point, I'm sure this poor woman was considering a career change. Anyway, we got the whole thing straightened out. Luckily running power tools sporadically for five months does not equate to a mountain of debt. The point is, though, that unknowingly we let this bill go for five whole months before anything happened.

I know so many people who grew up with strict guidelines that bills are to be paid promptly and that the squeaky wheel gets the grease (meaning: pay the bills that people are threatening you over first). Unfortunately, this is not in your family's best interest. This was an extremely difficult lesson for me to learn. It took my poor husband years to beat out of me the habit of paying the "bad people" first or of trying to pay everything I can as soon as I can scrape a few pennies together. Because you just never know what else is coming down the pike.

Have you ever heard the old adage (it's mostly said to small business owners) "pay yourself first"? I believe the same thing holds true for running a household. When I say I pay myself first, I consider taking care of the mortgage, utilities and groceries as paying myself. I know that no matter what else gets neglected or taken away, if I take care of those things every month, then my family is safe and well taken care of. No matter what is going on in our lives, I would never jeopardize my family's food, shelter and warmth. Everything else is gravy.

Now, of course, other companies don't like to hear this. They all want me to pay them first and now. And I'd like to, I really would. But I don't always have enough money to give everyone what they deserve. I try not to duck calls, I try to keep in touch and let people know what's going on and that they will, eventually, get their money. Some of them are very nice and patient (these are usually the other small, local businesses), but some of them get nasty - quickly.

They will try to convince me that my credit card, satellite television, cell phone or medical expenses are the most important things in my life and that I need to hop on over and hand them a nice juicy check, pronto. I know this is not true - even though I will still fret over it and probably be mean to my husband after dealing with these people on any given day - I know this is not true. The only truth is that we NEED our home, our food and our electricity - and that's really it, the rest can wait....if they HAVE to. And sometimes they do. I feel badly that we can't handle everything all the time, but as they say sometimes: poop happens. (Ok, so they don't usually say *that* exactly, but this is a family-type book.)

About a year ago, my younger son needed some dental work done, nothing as extensive as his brother's oral surgery, just little stuff. And the bill wasn't that much, somewhere in the neighborhood of $400.

While in the grand scheme of things, that's not a lot of money, it is something extra for the month and wasn't in our budget to give all at once. Our dentist knows us and so she agreed if I paid her what I could that day, she would bill me and I could pay the rest later.

Unbeknownst to me, however, this was at the beginning of our national economic crisis and work stopped trickling in, making it necessary for us to stretch our dollars even further. After receiving the dental bill, I was only able to send her $20, $30 or $50 every now and then - and even that small amount I couldn't do every month. She was patient....for a while. Then her receptionist started calling and I explained things to her and promised to send something in when I could and she kept billing me....and billing me...and billing me.

Now, honestly, I've emailed her (since I can't actually get her in person on the phone) a few times to offer to work off my debt or trade for it (she's the one with the side business I'd done some writing for to barter my bills in the past) and to let her know that I truly intend to pay off the bill, but need some patience and leniency. I've also spoken with her staff, on more than one occasion. But when, after about a year, the certified letter came, I started to get mad. At that point I'd paid the bill down to about $150. I was very disappointed that after trying so many times to work out an arrangement in a person-to-person way and getting no response at all she had the audacity to go the legal route.

At that point, I realized that she was quickly becoming like the other debt collectors (only I know her more personally and really like her, which only makes it that much more upsetting). But no matter how much I like her, I will never decide to pay her bill in full and leave my bank account too low to cover our mortgage, groceries and utilities. I immediately sent her another $30 check and continued to do so as best I could.

97

The big picture, to me, is that no matter who says what to me on the phone or in a certified or legal letter, I will always take care of my family first. There are no other expenses we could incur that would be more important than The Big Three (except, of course, bail - and he'd better come up with the money to spring me!).

As I said before, I've dealt with all kinds of debt collectors and I know the kinds of things they say to people. And I used to believe them. I was certain that when they said I HAD to make a payment over the phone that day or they'd start legal action or when they said I'd lose my home or when they said I would be sorry if I didn't work with them. The truth is - they are liars! (Except possibly if it's the mortgage company or tax agency threatening to take your home - they are possibly the only entities that have that authority.)

Debt collectors, I have come to realize, are really just lowly paid pencil pushers who are nothing more than glorified telemarketers. Their company gets paid more for every penny they can get people to pay in. And in many cases they just say whatever they can to scare people into making payments - even if it's not the truth. And they will keep after you. They call. They mail. Then they call some more. I've had different people from the same debt collection office call me ten times a day - and they all pretend they don't know that others have called or what they've offered. I've finally adopted the policy of insisting they send anything they have to say in writing and that they may never call the house again (this came after one of them got my son on the phone and proceeded to give him the third degree about what his daddy does for a living and where is he now and it went on until I overheard the conversation and snatched the phone away. My son also got a good lesson that day - I told him NO ONE is allowed to talk to him that way and that he should never answer those kinds of questions and then I gave him the right to hang up on anyone he doesn't know if they ask weird questions.)

Another thing I learned in dealing with debt collectors is that they often don't even work for the company you owe money to. Some companies have collection offices inside their businesses, but most others will write off what you owe them after a certain period of time as a "bad debt", which is a tax deduction to them, then they give the file to a totally different entity to see if they're interested in trying to pry your hard-earned money away from you. In these cases, you really don't owe the people calling you anything - they are totally separate from the company you were indebted to. These people are the worst hounds and really, aside from telling on you to credit agencies and bugging the snot out of you, there's nothing they can legally do to you. They didn't provide you with any goods or services, they've had no contracts or agreements made with you. The company you did owe money to wrote it off as bad debt and decided to wash their hands of you. When this happens, we usually decide to wash our hands of their hounds, too. For companies who truly try to collect money from you for debts you owe to them because of goods and services they've provided, we typically speak frankly with them and try to work out a resolution, but they have to be willing to give and take - to be patient, reasonable and open to compromise.

All too often I hear about families who have bought into the threats made by debt collectors and they make large payments to these companies, taking away from their savings and using their monthly budget in order to satisfy the bill collectors. Then they have nothing left for mortgage payments or anything else and before you know it they are losing their homes.

This happened to the daughter and son-in-law of some friends of ours. They had a very large amount of debt (I'm not sure of the amount) due to an emergency hospital stay and treatment for the daughter. When they couldn't pay their medical bills, the debt collectors got nasty and the couple caved. They used every penny they had to keep the debt collectors off their backs and then could not pay their mortgage payments. It only took a few short months for the mortgage company to foreclose on their house, leaving them homeless, helpless and ashamed.

A dear friend of mine is currently on the brink of a potentially devastating situation. Upon learning that she needed to have her gall bladder removed and had scheduled surgery she learned that her husband needed the same exact procedure. His was urgent so he went first and while he was recovering (or so they thought), she had her surgery.

Two days later she's up and running and he's still in bed in great pain. It turned out that he has pancreatic cancer and other problems that were keeping him from recovering. To go backward a bit, complicating the situation - the husband is the farm manager of a large cattle ranch. So now, the wife is facing mounting medical bills, trying to run the farm herself, having to spend much of her days running her husband to doctor's appointments and having to keep on the doctors about caring for her spouse properly (which they waver on depending on the day), not to mention running her household, keeping her job and taking care of their kids.

Needless to say, she's stressed to the hilt. One large concern that she has though (aside from obviously worrying about her husband's health), is that she keeps getting medical bills in the mail and she knows that there are only more and bigger ones to come as her husband continues his treatment.

My advice to her was - leave the bills: set them aside and worry about your family right now. If they start calling the house tell them your family is in the midst of a medical crisis that is taking all of your time and energy and in the meantime they need to go to hell. The MOST important thing is to take care of your family - period. Paying your bills IS important, don't get me wrong. I would never advocate just incurring expenses purposefully and intentionally ignoring the associated bills. BUT, in crisis situations the bills are not your main priority. My friend's main priority is to help her husband make decisions about his health and treatment, support him, assist him and make sure that her sons are also being taken care of.

In situations like this, if you have the money to cover your bills, but are too stressed with health concerns to deal with them, assign a more neutral third party to cover this duty temporarily. Maybe a sibling, grown child, parent or trusted friend could be in charge of collecting and sorting the mail and passing along the personal letters, tossing the junk mail and setting aside the bills. You might give that person a debit card to take care of your bills on-line or a checkbook with pre-signed checks and let them handle the stress of your bills for a while. Of course you'll need to make sure that you have the funds in the account to cover the bills or have your surrogate bill-payer just give you a monthly total each month for you to make a deposit to cover what they're about to pay. The last thing you need is the stress of bouncing checks to top it all off, so make sure that the two of you still communicate about the bills, even if it's only for that person to say "I need you to put $500 in your checking account by next Friday for this month's bills."

My friend is also concerned about her credit. If she doesn't keep on top of her bills and finances during this medical crisis and has to find a new place to live later on she wants her credit score to be decent so that she can get a loan. Well, yeah, having a good credit score is helpful for buying or renting a home. But it isn't essential and frankly, there are so many other ways your credit score can get screwed up without you even knowing about it, so there's nothing to say that it's ok right now anyway.

The main point is - these are the things bill collectors have already put into her head when really the only thing she should have to worry about right now is caring for her husband. The rest can wait.

Here's the thing. If you pay bills you can't afford to pay and neglect your mortgage, you WILL lose your house. If you neglect the extras (and this is everything other than The Big Three I mentioned) and keep paying The Big Three consistently, then you may make some people angry and you may be harassed by phone calls and litigious mail, but you will still have a roof over your head. Now, sometimes the people you owe money to will just continue to nag you ad infinitum, but sometimes (and I've found it has nothing to do with how much you owe, just who it is you're dealing with) they will proceed with legal action.

In many cases, the people you owe money to will have a judgment brought against you that says you owe the money and it will be a dirty little stain on your credit report (and, trust me, when you get to this boat, your credit score is wayyyyyyyy down low on your priority list), that will be with you for a decade. Sometimes, even, your debtholder will go all the way and sue you directly, causing you to hire a lawyer and present your case to a judge in person.

The most important thing to do at this point, is have documentation of your income: W-2's, prior tax returns, Balance Sheets, Profit and Loss statements, etc. and proof of your expenses utility bills, mortgage paperwork, auto loan paperwork, etc. - anything that is a regular monthly expense, including groceries, insurance, gas (ya gotta get to work if you are going to keep working and making this precious money everybody wants a piece of!).

What you want to do is prove, basically, that you can't get blood from a turnip! Also, it's best, I find, to be open-minded and somewhat agreeable. I think a judge will want to see that we *want* to pay our debts and that we are open to some sort of arrangement. Going to court, though, is really, to put it in Forrest Gump's words, like a box of chocolates: you never know what you're going to get! The case could be dismissed (yay!), or the judge may force you into some sort of payment arrangement (eh, okay), or he/she could force you into bankruptcy in order to pay the debts in bulk.

As far as I know, however, bankruptcy protects the primary residence of the parties involved - meaning you get to keep your home no matter what. I have known people who have filed bankruptcy and sold their home in order to come up with the money to pay the lawyers and debt-holders so that the situation ends more swiftly. I don't consider this optimal, unless you can get a lot of profit from your home and can afford something else that is appropriate and comfortable for you and your family with what's left after the bankruptcy expenses are paid. Anyone who goes down this route, however, is at least doing it on their own terms. They haven't been forced out of their home, they still either get to keep the house or sell it and have the profits to distribute to help with their debts.

I have no proof to offer, but I believe that every judge in ever district will be different - heck, even the same judge can make different decisions given his or her demeanor on any given day. But I would imagine that no judge, in his or her right mind, would force a person or family into homelessness for the sake of paying off medical expenses.

While debt collectors may, invariably, try to persuade me that I'll rue the day I turn down their "generous" offers, I know in my heart (and my brain) that I am always better off paying my mortgage, utilities, groceries and auto expenses first before deciding what funds are available for other obligations.

It's always best to stick to your priorities and don't let people who don't have your best interests in mind dissuade you from them.

Chapter 12: Living Well is the Best Revenge

Living well is the best revenge: pretty sage advice for such an old adage. Studies have shown that people who watch what they eat, exercise regularly and practice good living habits spend much less every year on medical costs than those who do not. It makes sense, really, that the better one takes care of oneself, the less medical treatment that person will need over their lifetime.

Diet and exercise combat so many bodily health problems and risks, like heart disease, cholesterol, high blood pressure, obesity and complications due to stress (just to name a very few). There are so many other easy decisions we make everyday that, if made well, can very positively affect our health, keeping us out of the doctors office. And isn't that really what we want? It doesn't matter what type of care is available or how much it costs if we never need it!

I have adopted so many natural remedies into the lives of my family, some for health reasons and others just because. And I truly believe we are such "hearty stock" because of our lifestyle and partly thanks to the good genes my parents and my in-laws passed down.

When I first became a parent, I was astounded at the stories other new mothers would tell about constant doctor visits, ER trips and prescription medications that their children required. (This, possibly, was why I was white as a sheet when my husband suggested dropping our health insurance when he did!) It seemed like every new friend I made had dozens of stories to tell about viruses and infections, aches, pains and ailments. I was starting to believe that motherhood was just a stepping stone to a career as a clinical nurse, which was nothing I had in mind.

I started to notice large differences between the lifestyles of the women I was listening to and myself. Nearly every other mother I met was a clean freak/germaphobe. They all had spotless homes (definitely me excluded) that smelled of a combination of bleach, antibacterial soap and ammonia mixed with a hint of Glade (as a cover, no doubt). Whenever we went out, they had contraptions to put in strollers and shopping carts so that their babies never touched any foreign surfaces. At regular intervals, when not in their own home, mommy was spotted swabbing down baby's hands and face with antibacterial baby wipes or hand sanitizer.

Not me. I was raised with the motto "Everybody needs their daily allotment of dirt" -so spoke my father every time my children got dirty, or he entered my not-so-tidy home. It was no big deal, my entire life, for anyone to get their hands dirty, touch a shopping cart - or anything else they dang-well pleased. My mother kept a nice house - I wouldn't say spotless, but nice. In fact I always remember my mother saying that she would never have passed her mother's meticulous white glove test. Luckily, that gene did not get passed down to my mother or myself.

Anyway, what I remember of those mothers I knew who repeatedly kept every germ and microbe at bay is that those were the mothers whose children suffered the most. Those were the families running to the doctor every few weeks with terrible coughs, ear infections, viruses and other medical problems.

I don't know if it's just wishful thinking on my part, but I always believed that by not being such a germaphobe my children were getting their fair share of daily dirt and thereby increasing their little systems' immunity to germs. That's the thing about illnesses - a tiny dose of illness or germs is easily battled and overcome by our bodies natural immune system. Having won these smaller battles, our bodies are thereby able to combat larger doses of germs and viruses. Which makes sense if you think about it - aren't many of the vaccinations we get for our children really just small doses of the viruses we are immunizing them against?

What I live by is basically, everything in moderation. I clean moderately, therefore my family is exposed to a moderate amount of germs. I believe that this increases our health factor some - not to mention decreasing my stress levels (housecleaning is the pits).

When the boys were little, I also heard of a study that stated that just a few minutes of time spent outside daily gives our bodies the amount of vitamin D we need. Ever since then, I've made sure we get a little extra. While my germ-freak friends were keeping their kids indoors (except for in and out of the car to get to the doctors!) or keeping them completely sun-blocked, fully-clothed and donning hats, my kids were always free to romp and roam, splish and splash in puddles, make mud pies and all sorts of nonsense they thought apt to get into. Again....in moderation.

We live in Virginia, where the summer sun can be quite intense and harmful to the skin and body, so when those "black flag" days come about I just make sure they aren't out for too long and that they have a moderate amount of sun-block on. I must admit, I'm a bit of a hermit, spending more time with my computer than my beautiful family or the great outdoors, but I do try to force myself outside a little each day as well.

I find it's pretty easy to get a bit of outside time without really interrupting my daily routine. When I have to run errands, I park in not-so-convenient spots, forcing myself to walk farther to get into the store (see - sunshine and exercise!). When my kids have after-school activities, instead of driving home and then back again to get them, I walk around the community or sit outside and read while I wait for them. My mailbox is about one-tenth of a mile from my house and just retrieving the mail is a great way to get a little extra sunshine and exercise, too.

It's just so easy, you see, to start doing such little things that increase our health. Luckily, it has a snowballing effect. I found that the more little things I forced myself to do to get some sunshine, also gave me a bit of exercise, too. Unluckily, my parents have been a bit overweight for as long as I can remember. And for as long as I can remember, my mother always complained about being overweight and all the complications it caused, like her lack of confidence, her body's discomfort, her weak hips, knees and foot arches, etc. But for as long as I could remember (until very recently), she never did a thing about it. Also, unfortunately, I was headed down that same path. Very fortunately, though, I have a wonderful friend who wasn't having any of that.

One day, my dear friend, Susan, snapped - she'd had it listening to me complain about how fat I was and she looked me straight in the eye and said, "I have been trying to get you to come with me to Jazzercise for a year now. If you don't like the way you look, then do something about it!"

So I did. It was the wake-up call I needed. I knew that she was right and that if I didn't do something I would wind up even more like my mother, overweight and in my sixties needing extensive treatment to help with my joints, bones, cholesterol, blood pressure and complete lack of pleasure with my body. At that point I was 182 pounds and teetering on the brink of a size 14. While I realize that this is the size of the average American woman, I also knew that this was not where I was comfortable.

I noticed a difference immediately after joining Jazzercise - unfortunately the difference was that the numbers on the scale were going UP! It was good weight, though - I could already feel my clothes fitting better, getting looser. The initial weight I had gained was muscle tone. Within about two months I noticed that I was losing more weight from fat than I was gaining with muscle and I started shedding the pounds nice and easy. I lost over thirty pounds that first year and it is still (after two years, now) coming off, just a bit more slowly. I am now down to 136 pounds and a size 7/8. I feel fantastic, look terrific and have tons more energy, confidence and know that my body, heart, joints, bones, etc. are thanking me.

Exercise can do so much for our health; boosts immunity, increases muscle, decreases fat, reduces stress, strengthens the heart, helps the brain run more efficiently and is a real mood elevator. I will always credit Jazzercise, my ever-wise friend Susan and my gorgeous friend Kim, who is my instructor and has the body I aspire to, with the state of my new body! Thank you, ladies!

I know not everybody can get into a program like Jazzercise. It costs money, which immediately has some people thinking that they could do the same thing for free on their own at home. I felt the same way. After I'd been there a few months, I no longer had the money to keep going and was about to drop out, when the aforementioned goddess Kim approached me and said she was about to become an instructor but needed a class manager. I asked what a class manager did and she explained the job (which is soooo easy, even I can do it) and ended with "and you get your workouts for free". No pause, I took it. I've been working out for free ever since.

There are all sorts of things anyone can do to get the exercise needed without it costing a cent, you just have to be creative sometimes. As I said before, I sometimes park at the far end of a shopping center lot and walk the extra distance into the store. Sometimes I walk around town while waiting for my kids to finish soccer practice, tae kwon do, etc. I walk up and down my driveway to get the mail or meet the school bus. And when I really need a boost, I pop in my ear buds and dance like a crazy woman around my house (preferably while no one is looking).

For some people, though, exercising is most effective as a group effort. I understand totally. Although I'm very motivated to do things like walk and dance when I'm alone, I'm most motivated when I'm in the midst of a group of women who are encouraging, supportive and upbeat and we can get together to exercise in a fun and effective manner. Exercise, despite some bad reviews, is actually lots of fun. You can do entertaining things like dance or play ball, but it's most enjoyable when you can see that it's actually working.

If you are one of those people who need people but you worry about the expense of joining a team, a club or a class, there are still ways that you can get what you need. You can always look for ways to do what I did - arrange a work for workout exchange. In my case I only have to work a few minutes before and after the classes I take - it's very convenient and the benefits to both me and the Jazzercise center are pretty equitable. There are other ways in which people at our center arrange for free workouts which might work at other Jazzercise or workout centers and clubs. We have babysitters who watch the kids during one class and then are able to take another class for free. We also have women who help with keeping up our website and marketing in exchange for free classes.

In some cases, gyms, clubs or other workout centers may require you to be an employee in order to get free memberships. For these you might have to put in a bit more time, like 10-20 hours a week.

In exchange, though, these types of jobs will pay you hourly in addition to your free membership. If you could use a little extra money, free workouts and have the time this is a great arrangement. Not only can you get these benefits, but you'll also be able to do a greater variety of things since these centers have a wider array of the type of help they need, from bookkeeping and other administrative needs to instructors and spotters to people to help keep the center and equipment clean.

This may be too much commitment for you, maybe you already work full-time or just don't have an extra 10 or 20 hours a week to give to a job. There's still more options. Community bulletin boards, on-line forums and other public domains are great places to post notices that you're trying to get a group together for exercising purposes. You should first check to see if someone else is already trying to put something like this together. If not, put up your own notice. You can make it whatever you're interested in doing: walking, jogging, biking, playing tennis or just looking for other people interested in exercising and you can get together and discuss what you'd like to do. It's very easy to find other people who want to exercise more, the problem is getting schedules together to do it. What does work is just randomly approaching people and telling them you're going to start taking your lunch break or your kids' sports practice time, etc. to go for a walk (or whatever you want to do to get moving). Generally other people that are around during those times (like coworkers, family members or other parents) will think it's a great idea and one or two will join here and there. You might have to get the ball rolling and do the activity alone the first few times, but usually when those around you see that you're committed to it a few will feel the inner-pressure to do it, too. It's how peer pressure works, only this time around you can use it to make positive things happen.

I know I started this chapter saying I do all kinds of things to keep my family healthy and all I've talked about so far is my neglectful cleaning skills, getting sunshine and exercise. But there's so much more.

I keep an herbal remedies and natural remedies resource book in the house. Anytime anyone has a problem, whether it's a cough, a wart, a rash or nosebleeds, I consult this book before doing anything else. It's amazing the sorts of things that are in this book. The first time I cracked it open I thought it was useless. I'd never heard of any of the things in there that they suggested - they looked like a bunch of foreign weeds and herbs to me. Little by little, though I familiarized myself with some of the things in there that I could easily identify. I noticed that it listed dandelions as an ingredient in remedies to serve as a diuretic, liver tonic, mild laxative, and to help clear up acne and eczema and much more. I read that the milk in the dandelion stem could help cure the wart on my foot - and it did.

I found a weed identified in the book as an aid for nosebleeds (which my younger son gets from time to time) in my yard. It's unbelievable, but it says you can just stuff a little flower from this yarrow weed in the nostril to help the bleeding stop. Then there's tea tree oil - which I'd never heard of, but I found a small bottle of it at Wal-Mart for just a few dollars. This stuff, which has a smell unlike any I've ever experienced, is like some sort of miracle tonic. It helps to treat acne, cold sores, cuts and scrapes, nits, warts, yeast infections and can even be used to make home cleaning products more effective.

Like I've said many times throughout this book, I consult the Internet often, for treatments as well as to find easy-to-make home remedies for things my family faces - like a rosemary infusion to add to my shampoo for thicker hair, breathing exercises for my son's coughing, stretching exercises for my pinched nerve and all sorts of things I would never have imagined on my own.

I believe in resourcefulness above all else and I love that I can help keep my family out of the doctor's office just by doing a little homework and combing my home and yard for natural ingredients. Additionally, I've taken to growing a little herb garden. St. John's Wort is a plant that helps with mood elevation, lavender helps with headaches, stiffness and sinus relief, chamomile helps with upset stomachs, etc. It helps to have these things on hand. During the summer months these hearty plants produce so much of the herbs that I can't possibly use them all, but during the winter, the plants go bare. In order to even out the odds, I cut the mature leaves of the plants all summer long and save them either by drying or freezing them so that I can use them in the colder months.

Some of the other things I do to keep my family healthy are just everyday common-sense things. I make sure the kids and I brush our teeth twice a day (the husband is on his own - even though I consider him to be like having a third child, truly I count on his adultness to kick in when it comes to his own hygiene). Nothing gets you to the dentist faster than kids not brushing well.

Since one of my boys is a master at deception (and the other is even more skilled than that), I've taken to doing random face-to-open-face inspections, whereby every so often I check their breath and peek at the pegs to make sure they have, in fact, been brushed. I also buy them fluoride mouth rinse to make sure they get enough of that, since we're on well water, although the dentist assures me that their twice-a-year fluoride treatments at her office are sufficient.

I must admit, I'm not a star when it comes to flossing, but I do advocate doing that regularly, too.

I make sure my entire family is eating well. Anytime one of my boys asks for a sugary or junk-food snack, if I say yes then I make sure the next thing they ingest is something healthy. It's a balance for sure, but I believe that for every pudding snack pack or handful of chips they eat they get a piece of fruit or cup of yogurt to counter it.

We also have very few restaurant and fast food meals. In fact, I've even grown suspicious of the cafeteria food served at the kids' school. It's not that I think their meals aren't nutritious (because I know that they are planned by professional nutritionists), but whenever I give the boys the go-ahead to buy lunch at school, they are tempted by the "extras" the school allows them to purchase. Nothing says sugar rush more than a 10- or 12-year old that's just been given the green light to buy a la carte. It makes me more than a little upset that the company running the cafeteria at the school feels it's okay to let elementary-aged children decide whether or not it's ok to buy fizzy drinks, cookies, chips and ice cream with their lunch. It's not that I have a problem with them having ONE of those items WITH their lunch, it's just that left to their own devices (which they are at school) they will pitch the lunch they've purchased and munch solely on the junk food they supplemented it with.

For that reason, I pack their lunches most days. After sandwiches, chips and fruit ad nauseum, my kids begged to start buying from the cafeteria again. So we worked out a compromise. I asked them what they would prefer to pack and surprisingly, they came up with a lot of healthy alternatives I never would have thought to put in their lunch boxes. Things like celery packed with peanut butter, slices of bologna and cheese with crackers, Thermoses of mac and cheese, yogurt tubes, peel-apart cheese sticks, fruit cocktail and much more graced their suggestion lists.

Now they don't mind packing lunch so much and to my joy, they are now the kids with the cool stuff everyone else wants to trade for.

One of the things that surprised me was that they really missed the school lunch because it was usually something hot, whereas my sandwiches are not. After they told me this I got them each a hot food storage container and started packing them soups, pastas, burritos, hot dogs, and other steamy goodness. Sometimes I get back a half a sandwich at the end of the day, but I never, ever get a half-full Thermos back - it always looks as if it's been licked clean.

The importance of this really is that I know what my kids are eating and it's a good balance of treats and healthy items.

I've tried to apply the same concept to our at-home meals as well. If everyone loves mom's cooking so much, they tend to beg to go out to eat a lot less. As it turns out, my older son is an even better chef than I am, so together we pioneer some tasty and unique meals, which I love so much. It's great spending time together in the kitchen and it's so nice to see someone enjoying their time in the kitchen (unlike me, who grumbles every time it comes time to deciding what to make for four people with unique palates).

By eating at home we save a lot of calories and fat intake. Even the healthiest of restaurant meals seem to be pretty high on the calorie and fat scale. In addition to trying to find different things to make at home, we try duplicating some of the things we love eating when we go out. We've mastered pizza, fried rice and steak salad (it may sound weird, but steak salad is the yummiest ever -promise!).

I know this isn't a recipe book, but I feel compelled to share steak salad with you now that I've brought it up. We found this delightful dish while spending a summer in Pennsylvania and once we'd spotted it, we found it on darn near every menu in the state. While it may be popular there, I've yet to see it in any other part of the country.

So, here's the deal - it's super easy. You make a salad, you grill steaks and you fry French fries. After everything's ready you build the meal in individual bowls or on plates. First go the French fries on the bottom. Then add the salad. On top of that are thin slices of steak, grated American cheese (if you freeze Velveeta for five minutes, you can actually grate it fairly easily), and then drizzle on some garlic ranch dressing.

Anyway, we eat pretty healthily and regularly. I try to cut off the deserts and snacks by 7:30 or 8 p.m. - after that it's fruit and water only. This gives the body more time to digest before bedtime. When the body is dormant food gets stored more easily as fat, since it's not getting burned off.

Okay, I'm starting to slobber on my keyboard - time for a new topic!

I frequently tell my husband that we seriously need to drink more. We've never really been alcohol drinkers. We can suck down a pitcher of iced tea at the drop of a hat, but we very rarely consume alcohol. In fact you can always tell if we've recently hosted a party at our house, because that's the only time you'll find alcohol in the fridge. After a month or two of swearing we'll drink it, I typically start combing my recipe books for recipes for beer bread, beer battered onion rings or shrimp, and stews, soups and casseroles that call for wine.

The truth of the matter is that a drink every so often really is beneficial, but many people over indulge. We have a friend who goes through a case of beer about every other day or so. This is not good. Incidentally, this friend also just had a nice little trip to the ER after nearly cutting off one of his fingers with a power saw in his workshop. Coincidence? Dunno.

Not only does a significant amount of alcohol cause you to gain weight, it also can make you have stupid accidents which can up your medical bills.

I have to admit, I do all of these things more for the benefit of my family and to teach my children a better way to take care of themselves than I do to save money and time on doctor's visits. But it's a great added benefit. I love the way my kids think about their bodies and their lifestyle because of the "weird" things their parents do at home. It really has expanded their minds and broken them out of the mold that their school and society strives so hard to cast them into. Every time I see them drag their video-obsessed friends outside to play or haul a bunch of ingredients out of the fridge and pantry to see what new dish they can make I know that they "get it" and that the things my husband and I have taught them about taking care of themselves and the ones they love are skills they'll carry with them wherever they go. And that, my friends, is worth more than any hospital could ever over-bill you for!

Chapter 13: On My Soapbox

When I first decided to write this book, I made a conscious decision to steer clear of the politics and social aspects of healthcare. I truly did not want to go into any of that *stuff* for many reasons. First of all I think it's all a bunch of hooey put out there by people who don't really care about the general population.

Second, those angles are a whole book all by themselves, and there's plenty of them out there already. I wavered after starting this book, thinking that I really should cover all the bases and include at least some stats, government program and initiative info in the chapters, etc. But after I began looking into it, it's really a never-ending chasm of a quagmirish enigma. It's also what can load a book down and make it so completely boring that you never could have made it this far without turning into Sleeping Beauty or Rip van Winkle.

Third, I really don't understand what's going on in the minds and actions of our government enough to speak out about it. THEY say they are doing this and starting up a program for that, but the problem is that by the time these things are batted about in congress and finally get approved, they are no longer what we the people thought they were. And by the time these programs, laws, initiatives, etc. trickle down to where they might do us some good they are so insignificant or complicated that they rarely benefit us anyway.

So, for the first 12 chapters of this book, I kept to my word, not uttering one syllable about the political or social aspects of healthcare. But then IT happened. I knew it would someday. In fact I sought it out knowing it was something I should experience. I saw Michael Moore's movie *Sicko*. It really wasn't anything I didn't know, but it was so in-my-face, saying, "This is what your book is about. This is what is happening to people who don't know how to take care of themselves. This is what is happening to people with AND without health insurance and the government is getting away with letting it happen over and over again."

I really took it personally, in fact that movie is partially responsible for the fact that although the first half of this book took me about two years to write, the second half (after watching the movie) has taken about two months. There's no getting away from it. The political and social aspects of healthcare cannot be a separate issue. For all of us in the United States, uninsured and insured alike, we need to present a united front and let our government and the healthcare industry know that we are aware and we're mad and we're not going to let them dictate our healthcare any longer.

I think the example in the movie that sticks out in my mind the loudest is the man who cut off two of his fingers with a power saw -

perhaps he reminds me of our friend, but regardless, it was so bad. His story, for those of you who haven't seen the movie, was that without health insurance he could not afford to have the doctor sew both of his fingers back on. One of the fingers could be saved for something like $12,000 and the other one would cost around $60,000. Since he couldn't afford both, he picked the cheap finger and went without the other finger.

Say what??? First of all, just because you don't have insurance doesn't mean that you are poor, so why was the doctor discussing fees and asking this man to choose a finger ahead of time? (I've got a finger for that doctor!) Now, perhaps the man asked about the fees, which is fine, but what on earth possessed this man (or his doctor, for that matter) to decide ahead of time that he could forego having the other finger re-attached? I've never heard of a doctor or hospital asking for payment up front. I've never heard of them asking for household income information or employment verification before admitting a patient.

There's no way that man should have had to choose over his fingers and no way a doctor should have asked him to. I really blame both people in this situation. Were that me or my husband the conversation would have been more like this:

Doctor: It's going to cost about $72,000 for me to re-attach your fingers.

Us: Whatever. Just do your job and fix my hand.

AFTER my fingers are sewn back on, THEN I worry about what it costs and negotiating with the doctor and the administrators about the price. No offense to the talented and scrupulous medical professionals out there, but they have an obligation to treat people who need help regardless of ability to pay. Even if they're in it for the money, they're SUPPOSED to be in it for the benefit of others.

I realize that this attitude is a little contrary to what I've said earlier in the book. Under normal, non-emergency situations I would definitely want to know what a treatment costs and discuss possible discounts. But in a situation like that, where time plays a major factor, I would never negotiate healthcare treatments before the treatment was administered. In this case, and many other examples, not getting treatment is not an option - and argue if you must, but going without one of my digits when it's right there in front of me and able to be reattached is NOT an option. Once you have your fingers sewn back on, you have a bit of leverage, no? See the doctor has all the leverage before the surgery - he has your fingers and you want them back. After the surgery, though, you have your fingers, which are rightfully yours in the first place and the doctor just wants money. Here's the balancing scales in front of you now: fingers......money......fingers......money. Which way do you think the scales are tipping? That's right - fingers way more important. And you can always negotiate price, you can always work out a payment plan or find ways to come up with money. But your window of opportunity for getting your fingers sewn back on and fully (or mostly?) functioning is pretty small.

I was blown away by the idiocy of this example in the movie, and trust me, there was so much more than that. Michael Moore went in search of healthcare for a few 9/11 heroes who were suffering from effects of spending so much time at Ground Zero yet who were shoved out of their jobs and off their medical plans. No one would cover them and they weren't getting the care they needed because it was too expensive to pay out of pocket. He found that the only place in the U.S. where there is socialized medicine is in our prisons. Our prisoners, including the foreigners who were residing at Guantanamo Bay, are entitled to full healthcare while incarcerated regardless of the nature of their crime, ability to pay (which, of course, they don't and aren't even asked to) or any other factors. Yet the people who risk their lives every day to truly serve our nation and it's citizens are completely overlooked.

After trying to take these heroes to Guantanamo Bay off the coast of Cuba to get U.S. medical treatment, they were ignored and turned away and they headed to Cuba. Now I don't know how much of this is the bare truth, but in Moore's documentary, the American heroes he took to Cuba were all treated at a Cuban hospital for free. They received medical exams, tests, treatments and medicine - all at no charge. Things they had suffered from that went untreated for years in the U.S. were handled in a matter of hours in Cuba. Why is that?

There's something totally wrong with that and with any administration who won't just jump in and change it - not little by little or over time or with the consent (and pork) of Congress, but right now, all at once - boom, done!

Well, we have an administration now who seems hell-bent on reforming our healthcare system and they have a **plan**. Although I am all for reform, and I am definitely in favor of having a plan, I am a bit skeptical.

I decided to go right to the source to find out the merits of this plan. On the President's own web site: www.barrackobama.com , his healthcare plan is spelled out as follows (as of 10/31/08) and I've given my two cents in parentheses and italics:

113

Plan for a Healthy America Barack Obama and Joe Biden's Plan

On health care reform, the American people are too often offered two extremes -government-run health care with higher taxes or letting the insurance companies operate without rules. Barack Obama and Joe Biden believe both of these extremes are wrong, and that's why they've proposed a plan that strengthens employer coverage, makes insurance companies accountable and ensures patient choice of doctor and care without government interference. *(Amen!)*

The Obama-Biden plan provides affordable, accessible health care for all Americans, builds on the existing health care system, and uses existing providers, doctors and plans to implement the plan. Under the Obama-Biden plan, patients will be able to make health care decisions with their doctors, instead of being blocked by insurance company bureaucrats. Under the plan, if you like your current health insurance, nothing changes, except your costs will go down by as much as $2,500 per year. If you don't have health insurance, you will have a choice of new, affordable health insurance options. *(Ok, red flag #1 -what if I don't want insurance, just affordable healthcare sans HMO?)*

Make Health Insurance Work for People and Businesses -Not Just Insurance and Drug Companies.

^ Require insurance companies to cover pre-existing conditions so all Americans regardless of their health status or history can get comprehensive benefits at fair and stable premiums. *(I like this stipulation, but who determines "fair and stable premiums" and how will we regulate them?)*

^ Create a new Small Business Health Tax Credit to help small businesses provide affordable health insurance to their employees. *(Could be good -makes sense.)*

^ Lower costs for businesses by covering a portion of the catastrophic health costs they pay in return for lower premiums for employees. *(I sense that this is like the bank bail outs where the government gives the banks billions of dollars in the hopes that they will then grant more loans, instead they scarf down the bucks and tighten lending further. I see the government subsidizing health costs for businesses and the businesses using that money for selfish board benefits instead of lower employee premiums.)*

^ Prevent insurers from overcharging doctors for their malpractice insurance and invest in proven strategies to reduce preventable medical errors. *(Sounds nice, but way too vague who regulates this? Who determines where to draw the line between charging and overcharging?)*

^ Make employer contributions more fair by requiring large employers that do not offer coverage or make a meaningful contribution to the cost of quality health coverage for their employees to contribute a percentage of payroll toward the costs of their employees health care. *(Again, just a tad vague look at the wording here: "more fair",*

114

"meaningful contribution", "quality health coverage", "a percentage of payroll". There definitely needs to be stronger, more defined language in this plan in order to be effective in any manner.)

^ Establish a National Health Insurance Exchange with a range of private insurance options as well as a new public plan based on benefits available to members of Congress that will allow individuals and small businesses to buy affordable health coverage. *(Ok, now I'm confused -is this for members of Congress or we, the little people? Are they saying that the public will now receive the type of health coverage that members of Congress now receive?)*

^ Ensure everyone who needs it will receive a tax credit for their premiums. *("everyone who needs it"? Isn't that just plain everybody?)*

Reduce Costs and Save a Typical American Family up to $2,500 as reforms phase in:

* Lower drug costs by allowing the importation of safe medicines from other developed countries, increasing the use of generic drugs in public programs and taking on drug companies that block cheaper generic medicines from the market *(Is it just me or have we learned nothing from our ecocrisis -wasn't shipping jobs overseas one of our largest complaints about why our economy is failing? How about making those cheaper drugs here and not overcharging for them?)*

* Require hospitals to collect and report health care cost and quality data

* Reduce the costs of catastrophic illnesses for employers and their employees. *(Okay, I'm beginning to doubt Obama's intelligence quotient. First of all you can't reduce the cost of an illness, you reduce the cost of the treatments and medicines -it doesn't cost you a dime to get sick, but it will likely cost you an arm and a leg to get better! I don't understand the correlation between me contracting a "catastrophic illness" and any increased cost for my employer -but they should definitely be helping me, the patient.)*

* Reform the insurance market to increase competition by taking on anticompetitive activity that drives up prices without improving quality of care. *(What is anticompetitive activity? And how do you make them compete?)*

The Obama-Biden plan will promote public health.

It will require coverage of preventive services, including cancer screenings, and increase state and local preparedness for terrorist attacks and natural disasters.

A Commitment to Fiscal Responsibility:

Barack Obama will pay for his $50 -$65 billion health care reform effort by rolling back the Bush tax cuts for Americans earning more than $250,000 per year and retaining the estate tax at its 2009 level.

Okay - it's just me now. To me, this plan for healthcare reform is merely a ploy to gain popularity. In essence Obama and Biden are proposing to change (slightly) the way that health insurance works. They want it to be more affordable to the public by making it more affordable to businesses. They want to purchase more prescription drugs from overseas than from domestic sources.

First of all, I must say, this is no reform. A reformation would mean that healthcare would significantly change (for the better, presumably) for a major percentage of our population. This plan is not that. This plan will be putting more money into major American companies in the hopes that they will make their subsidized premiums more affordable to their employees. In reality these large companies will say thank you, take the money and give their boards a nice little bonus. Not only will the government be handing over money to large domestic corporations in exchange for basically nothing, they will also be handing over wads of money to foreign drug manufacturers.

I see nothing in this plan that directly assists individuals. Instead of giving companies money and hope they lower premiums to their employees, why not just give the money to individuals to put toward their healthcare. Sure, not all of them will, but I bet a heck of a lot more Americans will use that money for healthcare on that plan than would be able to on Obama's plan which feeds the money through large corporations. The one thing I really don't think he gets (and I admit, I truly do want to believe that Obama is a good man with good intentions) is that wealth never trickles down - it bleeds up.

The healthcare situation in America is exactly the same as our economic situation. If you give the money to big business, it stays there and goes into the pockets of the big wigs. If you stimulate the individual citizens (us shmoes at the bottom), we save a little and we spend the rest, which will, in turn, trickle all the way up into those deep pockets at the top. But at least we get to choose and some of us might even save some of that money for ourselves or spend it in a way that enhances our lives while still letting it trickle upward. Ironically, as I am writing this, Obama is on the television (his daily appearance) speaking about his healthcare plan. He just commented that healthcare causes a bankruptcy in this nation every 30 seconds. May I make a recommendation? Mr. President, please read my book before you try to implement your plan!

In hopes of finding more defined parameters of Obama's plan, I scanned the Q and A section of the web site. There wasn't much in the way of concrete answers there either, but I found a few nuggets of encouragement:

(This excerpt was part of the response to how Obama's plan will help

small businesses afford to offer health insurance to their employees)

The Obama plan will also help employers that are unable to offer health coverage to their employees right now. The main reason employers do not offer health coverage to their employees is because it is simply too expensive. Obama's plan directly addresses the cost issue by allowing small employers to purchase a new public plan with subsidies for those who need it. For those who want private insurance, the Obama plan creates a National Health Insurance Exchange, which will act as a watchdog group and help reform the private insurance market by creating rules and standards for participating insurance plans to ensure fairness and to make coverage more affordable and accessible.

(I definitely like the watchdog idea -but who runs it? My guess would be another big business or government agency -either of which are laden with out-of-touch wealthy people who only know existence as part of the top 10%. While good in theory this has the shadings of a run-away train.)

Q. What if I am self-employed?

A. Then you know how hard it is for self-employed people to buy affordable health insurance today. Obama's plan will ensure that small businesses and those who are self-employed have affordable health care. Obama's new health plan will give individuals the choice of buying affordable health coverage that is similar to the plan available to federal employees and members of Congress or a private health insurance plan through an insurance market place known as the Health Insurance Exchange. The insurance will be affordable for all Americans and the insurance companies will not be allowed to deny you coverage or drop you because you get sick, the way they do now.

(This one may not apply to all of you, but it does particularly interest me, as a self-employed person, married to a self-employed small business owner. I have to say, again -I just don't get it. Who defines what is "affordable" and how will they regulate this exchange or public plans to keep them from raising insurance premiums annually, as most do?)

Here's the big issue that sticks in my craw: why does Obama feel that we all NEED health insurance? That's not the real issue here. With about 15 percent of the nation living without health insurance, why does everyone jump to the conclusion that we all WANT it and will jump at the chance to spend our money on it, if it only cost less? The real issue here is affordable and quality HEALTHcare - not INSURANCEcare!

What really irks me these days is listening to President Obama morphing and defining his healthcare reform plan and turning it into, not more affordable insurance for the masses, but now it's becoming a directive to REQUIRE every American citizen to have health insurance. I find this completely offensive. Yes, I live in a country where I am required to have driver's/automobile insurance and for some reason I can live with that. Why? Because if I'm reckless and hurt someone I'm covered. Because if someone else is reckless and hurts me or my family, I'm covered. But, as for my healthcare, my insurance status does not directly impact anyone else's health (outside of my own family) - it's my own business. If I want or don't want insurance, that's up to me and my husband. What will happen if we're all required to purchase health insurance? For one thing, not everyone can afford it. Obama says his plan will make it affordable. Frankly if everyone in the nation is going to have to have it, it will have to be free, because no matter how "affordable" it is, there will still be people who can't afford it. And then what happens when renegade rule-breakers like me decide we just plain don't want it, regardless of affordability and threat of punishment? It's just ridiculous and it's more of Big Brother telling us what to do, how high to jump and seriously, it's just another tax. I say this because part of this plan is to require people who don't purchase health insurance to pay the government a fee with their annual tax return. It seems to me that instead of finding a way to help such a large group of people, Obama has found a way to make more tax dollars from those people - that's not assistance, that's extortion.

I don't care how much or how little insurance costs, what I want to see are reasonable rates on doctors visits, prescription medications, ER trips, hospital stays, medical procedures, illness treatments, etc. If those costs were regulated by some virtuous watch dog, then none of us would need insurance at all.

I think that if Obama gets his way with this plan, the way it stands right now, our economy will continue to delve into the depths of despair. He will give major corporations money to subsidize employee health benefits, outsource our pharmaceutical needs to foreign companies and attempt to make everyone join an HMO. In response to this, the cost of medical care and drugs will actually increase while the HMO's and public plans will be heavily regulated so that they remain "affordable". With costs rising and premiums kept at all-time lows, the HMO's will soon be filing for government bail-outs, too.

If all of that continues, then eventually the HMO's will give way to the public plans and "exchanges" that are run by the government. Isn't this just a round-about way of nationalizing healthcare? If so, why not just call it what it is and implement that plan directly instead of spending billions of dollars on a plan that will eventually decline into nationalization and then chasing that with billions more dollars to reform the system again to make nationalization work? What if, right now, we get Obama to withdraw his plan and start anew. What if he were to just declare every health insurance company is now a vessel of the U.S.

government and all citizens of the U.S. are divided equally among them. Each HMO would then become a watch dog of the healthcare system, ensuring that all Americans get quality care at regulated affordable pricing, or better yet, for free. You know we're all going to be paying more in taxes (even if the government won't admit it) to pay for the bank bail-outs, the automobile industry bail-outs and Obama's stimulus package - so why not just use our taxes for us. Let the banks fail. Let the automobile industry fend for itself. Take the money we are already paying you (I'm talking directly to the government now) and the money we will continue to bleed for you and use it to offer us free and affordable healthcare with the HMO's working *for* us instead of against us.

I can't say that at any other time in my life I would be jumping all over nationalization of any sort of enterprise, but it just seems to be the way we're headed anyway. I grew up in a very patriotic household. You were a fan of the President just because he was YOUR president. Period. You supported him and believed in him and did whatever he mandated you do. Period. I can't even count the number of times I heard my father tell me or anyone else who seemed down on America how this is the greatest nation on the globe. Period.

That being said, I am a firm believer in competitive capitalism/market economy as well. I believe that everyone has the right to start a business or make money in any legitimate way they can and that if they can't compete or keep up, that business will fail and they will have to start over or concede and go to work for someone else. And I do believe we live in a great nation.

However, I am also a realist, a pragmatist, and a skeptic. I am wary of any government program, especially after they took advantage of our liberties following 9/11. I prefer government leave the people to themselves, or at least to their state. I think what went off-kilter, for me, is that today it seems that the only thing more evil than the abusive power of our federal government is the abusive and indulgent behavior of American big business.

It seems the older I get (and trust me, I try not to get any older at all), the more I wish for things to revert to the antebellum period. Well, some things. I like the idea that each individual and family was basically responsible for every aspect of their lives and that they were so far removed from the federal government because everything was so remote. Travel was slower and less efficient, communications were whatever you can think of that's slower than a snail and everything was fairly dependent on local conditions. Towns and communities banded together, not for the occasional misplaced family or social crisis, but on a daily basis, just because they were neighbors with similar interests and comparable conditions. In that era, one or two doctors would serve an entire community. That person knew everything there was to know about everyone in their town, from their health issues to their income and social status....and it didn't matter. They helped no matter what. They became doctors because science intrigued them and the idea of helping people was an obsession and if they got paid cash money, that was just icing. Barter was a normal, acceptable and expected part of doing business.

Those are the things I want for my children, which I guess is partly the reason we live in a tiny community out in the country. As small a community as we are though, the world is closing in on us; it pores in through our computers, our televisions, radios and newspapers.

Healthcare is not the only issue riding on our heels, but it just may be the one closest to tripping us up and causing us to land on our faces. We can only do so much at once, let's work together to fix our healthcare system. The very first step is to take responsibility for our own health care. Whether you have health insurance or not, research everything before you make a decision or let your doctor or hospital make a decision for you, read over your medical bills and invoices, negotiate when you can, but be sure that you are getting what you pay for and that you're paying for no more than you received. If we all act like watch dogs, we can affect the entire system and reduce costs for everyone in it.

APPENDIX A

DEPARTMENTS OF HEALTH AND DOCTOR PROFILE/LICENSE LOOKUP WEB SITES -BY STATE

** Each listing has 1) state name, 2) department of health web site address and 3) doctor profile or license lookup site link - in that order.

Alabama: http://www.adph.org/
    http://www.albme.org/Default.aspx?Page=PhysicianSearch
Alaska: http://www.hss.state.ak.us/
    http://www.docboard.org/ak/
Arizona: http://www.azdhs.gov/index.htm
    http://www.azmd.gov/profile/getlicense.aspx
Arkansas: http://www.healthyarkansas.com/
    https://www.armedicalboard.org/licenseverf/
California: http://www.cdph.ca.gov/Pages/default.aspx
    http://www.medbd.ca.gov/lookup.html
Colorado: http://www.cdphe.state.co.us/
    https://www.doradls.state.co.us/alison.php
Connecticut: http://www.ct.gov/dph/site/default.asp
    http://www.ct.gov/dph/cwp/view.asp?a=3121&q=389526&d
phNav_GI D=1821&dphPNavCtr=|#47137
Delaware: http://www.dhss.delaware.gov/dhss/
    https://dpronline.delaware.gov/mylicense%20weblookup/Search.aspx
Florida: http://www.doh.state.fl.us/
    http://ww2.doh.state.fl.us/IRM00profiling/searchform.asp
Georgia: http://health.state.ga.us/
    http://medicalboard.georgia.gov/00/article/0,2086,26729866_
2 6733429_43681190,00.html
Hawaii: http://hawaii.gov/health/
    http://pvl.ehawaii.gov/pvlsearch/app
Idaho: http://www.healthandwelfare.idaho.gov/
    http://idacare.org/
Illinois: http://www.idph.state.il.us/
    https://www.idfpr.com/applications/professionprofile/(X(1)S(
qv3n2i45exqiv045juvu5eut))/Default.aspx?AspxAutoDetectCookieSup port=1

Indiana: http://www.in.gov/isdh/
    https://extranet.in.gov/WebLookup/Search.aspx
Iowa: http://www.idph.state.ia.us/
    https://eservices.iowa.gov/licensediniowa/
Kansas: http://www.kdheks.gov/
    http://www.docboard.org/ks/df/kssearch.htm
Kentucky: http://chfs.ky.gov/dph/default.htm
    http://web1.ky.gov/gensearch/
Louisiana: http://www.dhh.state.la.us/
    http://www.lsbme.louisiana.gov/apps/verifications/lookup.aspx
Maine: http://www.maine.gov/dhhs/index.shtml
    http://www.docboard.org/me/df/mesearch.htm
Maryland: http://www.dhmh.state.md.us/
    http://www.docboard.org/md/df/mdsearch.htm
Massachusetts: http://www.mass.gov/dph/
    http://profiles.massmedboard.org/Profiles/MAPhysician-
Profile-Find-Doctor.asp
Michigan: http://www.michigan.gov/mdch
    http://www.dleg.state.mi.us/free/default.asp
Minnesota: http://www.health.state.mn.us/
    Https://www.hlb.state.mn.us/BMP/DesktopModules/ServiceF
o rm.aspx?svid=30&mid=176
Mississippi: http://www.msdh.state.ms.us/
    http://www.msbml.state.ms.us/physiciantracking.htm
Missouri: http://www.dhss.mo.gov/
    https://renew.pr.mo.gov/licensee-search.asp
Montana: http://www.dphhs.mt.gov/
    http://app.mt.gov/lookup/
Nebraska: http://www.hhs.state.ne.us/
    http://www.nebraska.gov/LISSearch/search.cgi
Nevada: http://dhhs.nv.gov/
    http://medboard.nv.gov/default.asp
New Hampshire: http://www.dhhs.state.nh.us/
    http://pierce.state.nh.us/MedicineBoard/disclaimer.asp
New Jersey: http://www.state.nj.us/health/
    http://www.msnj.org/pf/index.html
New Mexico: http://www.health.state.nm.us/
    http://www.docboard.org/nm/
New York: http://www.health.state.ny.us/
    http://www.nydoctorprofile.com/welcome.jsp
North Carolina: http://www.ncdhhs.gov/
    http://www.ncmedboard.org/Clients/NCBOM/Public/Public
M edia/find.htm
North Dakota: http://www.health.state.nd.us/

http://www.ndbomex.com/SearchPage.asp
Ohio: http://www.odh.state.oh.us/
     https://license.ohio.gov/lookup/default.asp
Oklahoma: http://www.health.state.ok.us/
     http://www.okmedicalboard.org/display.php?content=md_sea
rch_advanced:md_search_advanced
Oregon: http://oregon.gov/DHS/ph/index.shtml
     http://www.bme.state.or.us/search.html
Pennsylvania:
     http://www.dsf.health.state.pa.us/health/site/default.asp
     http://www.licensepa.state.pa.us/
Rhode Island: http://www.health.state.ri.us/
     http://www.docboard.org/ri/df/search.htm
South Carolina: http://www.scdhec.net/
     https://verify.llronline.com/LicLookup/
South Dakota: http://doh.sd.gov/
https://www.sdbome.com/LicenseVerification/LicenseVerificationLogi
n900.cfm?Redirect=%2FLicenseVerification%2Findex%2Ecfm
Tennessee: http://www.state.tn.us/health/
     http://health.state.tn.us/licensure/index.htm
Texas: http://www.dshs.state.tx.us/default.shtm
     http://reg.tmb.state.tx.us/OnLineVerif/Phys_NoticeVerif.asp?
Utah: http://hlunix.ex.state.ut.us/
     https://secure.utah.gov/llv/llv
Vermont: http://healthvermont.gov/
     http://healthvermont.gov/hc/med_board/profile_search.aspx
Virginia: http://www.dhp.state.va.us/
     https://secure01.virginiainteractive.org/dhp/cgi-
bin/search_publicdb.cgi
Washington: http://www.doh.wa.gov/
     https://fortress.wa.gov/doh/hpqa1/Application/Credential_Se
ar ch/profile.asp
Washington, D.C.: http://dchealth.dc.gov/doh/site/default.asp
     http://app.hpla.doh.dc.gov/weblookup/
West Virginia: http://www.wvdhhr.org/
     http://www.wvdhhr.org/wvbom/licensesearch.asp
Wisconsin: http://www.dhfs.state.wi.us/
     http://online.drl.wi.gov/LicenseLookup/IndividualCredential
S earch.aspx
Wyoming: http://www.health.wyo.gov/
     http://www.docboard.org/wy/

APPENDIX B

Sample Hospital Bill #1

** This was a real hospital's sample bill that I found on the Internet - with the names and contact information cleverly removed to protect the innocent. Me.

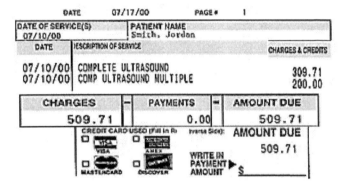

124

APPENDIX C

Sample Hospital Bill #2

** Again any real names and contact information has been strategically obscured.

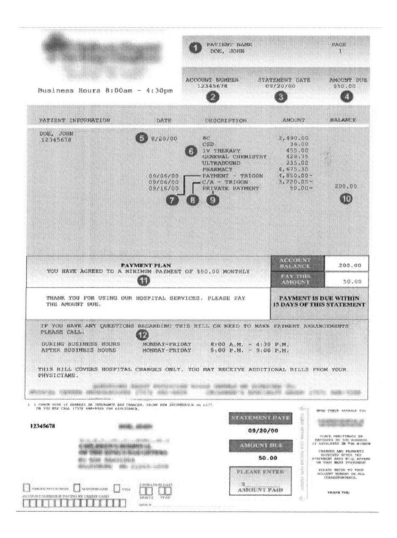

APPENDIX D

Sample Hospital Bill #3
(page 1)

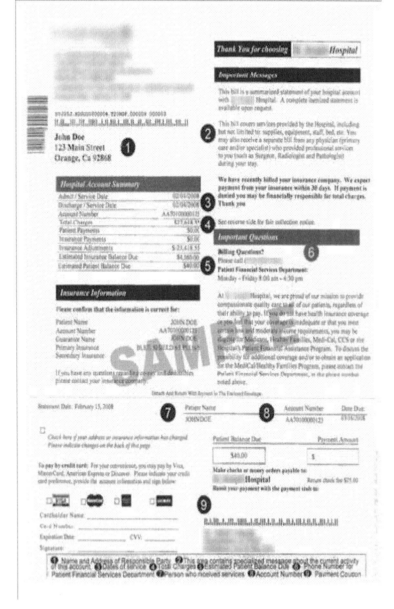

Statement Date: 02/15/2008
Account Number: AA7010000012
Discharge Date: 02/04/2008

Patient Services Provided - Itemized Charges

Summarized Detail

Services and Charges

Room and Care	$6,273.00
Pharmacy	$4,387.30
Central Services Supplies	$1,529.22
Laboratory	$2,366.81
Pathology	$518.68
Radiology - Diagnostic	$800.61
Operating Room Services	$7,524.00
Anesthesia	$682.50
Respiratory Services	$1,600.56
Recovery Room	$1,701.00
EKG/ECG	$424.87
Total Charges	**$27,618.55**

Payments and Adjustments as of 02/15/2008

Patient Payments	$0.00
Insurance Payments	$0.00
Insurance Adjustments	$-23,618.55
Estimated Insurance Balance	$4,160.00
Estimated Patient Balance Due	$40.00

Made in the USA
Lexington, KY
15 February 2010